Richard Loseby was born in Port Moresby, Papua New Guinea, in 1963. He grew up in Australia before moving to New Zealand at the age of eight. In 1980 he ventured into advertising as a copywriter, working in London from 1985 to 1993 before returning to Auckland, where he now works as a Creative Director at ad agency Ogilvy & Mather. He has two previously published and acclaimed travel books, *Blue is the Colour of Heaven* and *Looking for the Afghan*. Richard is married with two children.

A BOY OF
CHINA

RICHARD LOSEBY

HarperCollinsPublishers

For Tom and Issie

HarperCollins*Publishers*
First published in 2016
by HarperCollins*Publishers* (New Zealand) Limited
Unit D1, 63 Apollo Drive, Rosedale, Auckland 0632, New Zealand
harpercollins.co.nz

Text and photographs copyright © Richard Loseby 2016

Richard Loseby asserts the moral right to be identified as the author of this work. This work is copyright. All rights reserved. No part of this publication may be reproduced, copied, scanned, stored in a retrieval system, recorded, or transmitted, in any form or by any means, without the prior written permission of the publisher.

HarperCollins*Publishers*
Unit D1, 63 Apollo Drive, Rosedale, Auckland 0632, New Zealand
Level 13, 201 Elizabeth Street, Sydney NSW 2000
A 53, Sector 57, Noida, UP, India
1 London Bridge Street, London, SE1 9GF, United Kingdom
2 Bloor Street East, 20th floor, Toronto, Ontario M4W 1A8, Canada
195 Broadway, New York NY 10007, USA

National Library of New Zealand cataloguing-in-publication data:

Loseby, Richard, 1963–
 A boy of China : in search of Mao's lost son / Richard Loseby.
 ISBN 978-1-77554-088-5 (paperback)—ISBN 978-1-77549-125-5 (ebook)
 1. Loseby, Richard, 1963– —Travel—China. 2. China—Description and travel.
 I. Title.
 915.104—dc 23

Cover design by HarperCollins Design Studio
Front cover images: Boy © Robert Wallis/CORBIS; background by Blackstation/Getty Images
Back cover image: Garze © Richard Loseby
Typeset in Baskerville MT by Kirby Jones
Printed and bound in Australia by Griffin Press
The papers used by HarperCollins in the manufacture of this book are natural, recyclable product made from wood grown in sustainable plantation forests. The fibre source and manufacturing processes meet recognised international environmental standards, and carry certification.

As for me, I am tormented by an everlasting itch for things remote.
  Herman Melville, 1844

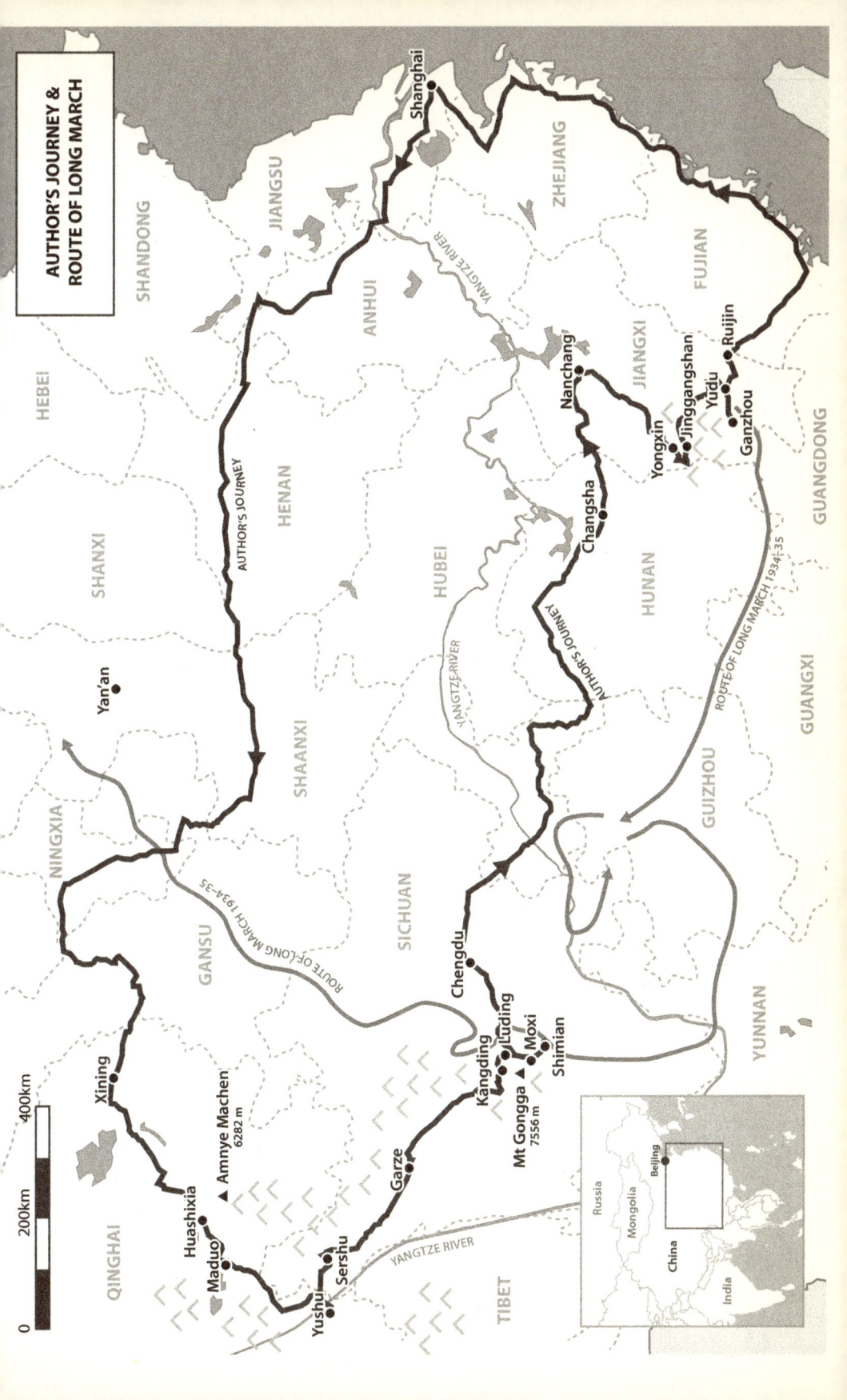

PROLOGUE

Beijing, 1949

He Zizhen, third wife of Chairman Mao, clasped and unclasped her hands anxiously as she peered from the windows of China's Communist Party headquarters. A grey winter sky hung low over Beijing's rabbit warren of ancient cobbled lanes and humble timber dwellings, where the inhabitants of her husband's new China huddled round mah jong tables and desperately gambled for scraps of food. Loyalists of the former ruler, General Chiang Kai-shek, had already been arrested and their bodies hung lifelessly from street posts and city gates, swaying in the icy wind that blew down from the Mongolian steppe. A wary population pointed fingers of suspicion in any direction, seeking to avoid becoming the focus of the Communist Red Army guards. They had good reason: the guards were young radicals, fired up by Mao's speeches, which denounced the old ways and promised them a brighter future in which their militant voices would be heard. These were dangerous times. Close neighbours and even family members looked nervously at each other over their half-empty rice bowls.

Not far away was the Forbidden Palace: dormant, emperor-less, devoid of the officials, concubines and eunuchs that once inhabited its many thousands of rooms. Little did He Zizhen care for history. What mattered most was the present, and that her world had now shifted on its axis in the most terrible of ways. Her husband Mao Tse-tung's infidelity with the actress Lan Ping had long since destroyed their marriage, but now word had come of something far worse. Her beloved sister had disappeared in a province many thousands of kilometres away to the south, while on a mission to look for the young son He Zizhen had been forced to give up years before, at the beginning of what had become known as the Long March. A father who cared more for power than his progeny, Mao had forbidden He Zizhen to travel there herself. Now, with her marriage over, and her life unravelling, she was tortured by guilt, grief and not knowing.

Within the tight circle of Mao's advisors, from which she was increasingly excluded, she could hear whispering that a madness had overtaken her. The murmurings were becoming stronger too, counselling 'him' that there were other places better able to care for her, places far away and out of sight that could tend to her worsening mental condition. Perhaps they were right. The loss of her child, her 'Little Mao', whom she loved with all her might and feared she would never hold again, was a weight on her heart that was beyond unbearable. Whatever strength of hope she had left now deserted her. Whatever life she'd imagined for them all was gone.

Her husband's officials said her son was a boy of China now: not hers or any other individual's, but a citizen who would grow to help make this new nation great through hard work on the land. It would be a noble life, a victorious existence, not in the arms of his birth mother, but in the warm embrace of Mother China.

'He Zizhen, you should rejoice and be proud,' they said.

But whenever she tried to feel that way, the tears would come and not stop. And nothing could be done to stem their flow.

ONE

It was while travelling through the more remote regions of western China, towards the end of 1989, that I first heard the strange story of Little Mao. I had entered the country from Northern Pakistan after travelling by foot across Afghanistan from Iran, arriving on the Chinese border just before an early snowfall closed the towering Khunjerab Pass. From there I had made my way to the horse-trading town of Kashgar in Xinjiang province, and an eventual encounter one Sunday with Mr Wong, the local schoolteacher.

Mr Wong was a thin, wiry figure in his thirties who wore grey suit trousers and a white business shirt through which a singlet was clearly visible. On his feet were sandals that showed off an assortment of unsightly toenails. He hated Kashgar and thought the local children dirty.

'Uighurs,' he said disparagingly, referring to the local population of ethnic Muslims. 'They use their hands to wipe their bottoms.'

His real home was thousands of kilometres away to the east in Hunan province, but Mr Wong had upset a Communist Party official there and had found himself 'relocated' to the far west 'for the good of the state'. I asked him what he had done to deserve such treatment and initially he wouldn't say, but the loose tongue that had got him into trouble in the first place was still active in his mouth. Over the next few hours, as we sat slurping Chinese tea in an outdoor restaurant beside a dusty street, Mr Wong described how he, personally, felt that the official story of the famous Long March was seriously inaccurate.

'Communist history is full of lies,' he whispered.

This was either very brave or very foolish. Questioning the official line on this historic event was always going to end in tears, for the Long March was portrayed as a key episode in the Civil War between the government forces of Chiang Kai-shek and Mao's Communist Party. To dispute its authenticity was tantamount to questioning Mao himself, who had personally overseen and contributed to its written account.

What was true was that, after a great deal of political strife and violent skirmishes against Chiang Kai-shek and his Nationalist government's regime, the Chinese Communist Party was born in 1931 in Jiangxi province, in southeastern China. In reply, Chiang Kai-shek sent wave upon wave of what he called 'annihilation forces' to wipe it out. For three years, the Communists held the Nationalists at bay, until the fledgling Communist Red Army found itself surrounded, pinned down in the mountains of Jiangxi. However, after the Nationalists launched one final, powerful offensive involving 500,000 troops, Mao and the Communists managed, in October 1934, to break free of this blockade and secretly flee their southern bases. The plan was first to escape, then eventually meet up with other Communists in the northern provinces of Gansu and Shaanxi. This tactical retreat became known as the Long March, even though it was not one march, but several, made up of different armies at first pushing westwards, then to the north. Some 100,000 people set out, but fewer than 10,000 made it to the finish. Those men and women, including high-ranking Communist officials and their wives, endured snow-covered passes, treacherous swamps, raging rivers and, of course, the armies of General Chiang Kai-shek, which pursued them relentlessly. The march lasted 368 days and covered 9,650 kilometres, ending in Shaanxi province. In all, 24 rivers were crossed, 18 mountain ranges were climbed and 11 provinces were traversed before the journey finally finished on the edge of the Gobi Desert in the caves of Yan'an, a location that would become the Communists' main base for the next 13 years.

In a Party conference speech in 1935, soon after the march had ended, Mao called the Long March a manifesto that had shown the Red Army to be heroes, a propaganda force that pointed the way to liberation, and a seeding-machine that would yield a great harvest across all of China.

Clearly that seed hadn't reached Mr Wong, whose doubts were almost certainly well founded. The Party is now known to have embellished many parts of the story of the Long March in order to depict it as a glorious moment in China's nationhood. The Battle of Xiang River in Guangxi, fought in the early part of the march, is one such event with a slightly embroidered history. Though a battle in which the Communists lost tens of thousands of men, it was painted as a victory where those soldiers had sacrificed their lives, paying the ultimate price in order to allow their fellow marchers to escape. In actual fact, it is now thought that at least half of them simply deserted. Many of Mao's armed forces had been forcibly recruited and so, facing the vastly superior forces of Chiang Kai-shek, they had shouldered their rifles and made a run for it. Not that you would know that from the official description of this particular battle. Clearly, Mao was never one for letting the facts get in the way of a good story.

In truth, the Long March was almost a terrible failure, with Mao's military mistakes along the way costing thousands of people their lives, through starvation and disease, in some cases as a result of his own unbridled political ambition. For instance, any regiments Mao suspected of not being entirely loyal to him, or perhaps maintaining allegiances to other Communist Party generals, he despatched through swamps that could have been avoided or made backtrack many hundreds of kilometres, just to break their spirit.

'Chairman Mao says he walked the whole way, but I know better,' said Mr Wong virtuously. 'The Leader was carried on the backs of soldiers he treated like slaves. He never cared for people, not even his own children.'

This was dangerous ground. No matter how far west you go in China, no matter how far from Beijing you travel, you just don't demean Mao Tse-tung. You might as well walk up to a Red Guard and stick your finger up his nose. Talk like this made me nervous. But Mr Wong was not about to stop and what he said next caught my full attention.

'You know of course, the sad story of Little Mao?'

The person Mr Wong was referring to was one of Mao's sons, Mao An Hong, who became affectionately known as 'Little Mao' because he looked so like his father. Mr Wong recounted that the boy was born in 1932, four years after Mao met his future third wife, He Zizhen, in the Communist stronghold of Jinggangshan. This secret mountain fort was surrounded by thick forests that enabled the Communists to mount many successful attacks on Nationalist forces, then disappear back into the jungle. Mao and He Zizhen were introduced to each other by a friend of He Zizhen's brother. Partly because she was well known as a brave fighter, a crack shot with a rifle (her nickname was 'the Two-Gunned General') and a devout Communist, Mao was smitten, and they married soon after. He Zizhen would eventually have six children by him, three boys and three girls. Only one, however, Li Min, who was born in 1936 after the Long March ended, survived to adulthood. Tragically for He Zizhen, the other children either died in childbirth or were compulsorily given away.

Because the Communists were often on the run, Mao and other senior leaders deemed a crying child a security risk, as the sound might give away their position. When Mao An Hong was just two years old, Mao and He Zizhen were forced to set off on the Long March. He Zizhen had no option but to leave Little Mao with local villagers, whom she no doubt hoped would stay behind and be spared harsh treatment by the chasing government soldiers. But by the time the Civil War was over and the Communists had gained control of the country, Mao and He Zizhen had lost all contact with their son.

Later, in 1949, continued Mr Wong, He Zizhen desperately searched for any information on Little Mao, but to no avail. Her sister tried to help, and on hearing of a child who matched his description in a town called Ruijin in Jiangxi province, hurried to the area — only to perish in a car crash en route.

He Zizhen never recovered from these tragedies, and suffered mentally as a result, spending many years in institutions in China and the Soviet Union. During one such absence, Mao declared his marriage to He Zizhen over and wed his fourth wife, the politically ambitious former actress Lan Ping. More famously known as Jiang Qing, she would later become the leader of the notorious Gang of Four.

For Mr Wong, all of this was proof of the dubious character of Chairman Mao. The fact he never bothered helping in the search for his son was unforgivable.

'A son is very important in Chinese society,' he said. 'To lose one is careless. The ancestors would be angry.'

After that I didn't see Mr Wong again, but his story of the lost boy stayed with me for a long time. Gradually my interest faded, partly because of the lack of real information, partly because I was busy working on other projects. But then, 17 years later, it was rekindled in the most unexpected of ways.

TWO

IT WAS BAKING HOT AND AIRLESS IN BANGKOK. THE ENTIRE population was waiting for the rains to arrive and provide some respite from the boiling furnace that this concrete city had become. Once upon a time there were trees lining the streets, but in the rush to modernise many had been cut down, leaving little in the way of shade from the burning sun. Town planners had begun to plant replacements, but these were no more than shoulder high and would take years to grow to their full height. From my office on the forty-third floor of the Empire Tower, I could see out over the city towards the west, where the monsoon still lurked off the coast of India in the Bay of Bengal. It was there: building, broiling, waiting for its moment to charge east and envelop us. Perhaps in a week or two it would come, but for now the searing sun and 40-degree temperatures were a daily burden.

I was in Thailand on a month-long contract with a large international advertising agency, whose job, on behalf of a client, was to launch anti-dandruff shampoo in China. The endless millions of Chinese office workers who had dandruff constituted an attractive and relatively untapped market, and major European shampoo brands were readying themselves to enter the fray.

It was in this capacity that I came to meet quite a few Thai of Chinese extraction. Many were the children or grandchildren of those who had escaped the political instability of China in the 1930s, often fleeing by boat and braving the South China Sea in order to reach the relative safety of what was then called Siam. One of them was Li, our agency receptionist. An attractive woman in her early thirties, Li was unmarried as yet, much to the distress of her mother, who was ever hopeful and sent a steady stream of willing suitors in Li's direction. Li took all of this in her stride; it was her duty, after all. But she viewed the prospective husbands with little enthusiasm. They were never her type. They were usually too fat, too old, too poor or too ugly. Sometimes, one might pass muster and we would hear about him the next day. But even the most promising of potential partners had one fateful flaw: they were all men. Li's tastes lay elsewhere, though she could never admit that to her parents.

It was, however, one of her male admirers who was to rekindle my interest in Mao's lost son. Chen, the man in question, was rich, he was handsome, he was even quite tall. He was a successful businessman and more besides: his number-one claim to fame, and no doubt his trump card in the boardroom, was that his family, purportedly, was closely linked with a number of high-ranking Communist Party officials from the early days — something akin to being related to royalty.

He came to the agency one Friday night when the boss was away and the caps were taken off the most expensive whisky bottles in the agency bar. The mood was ebullient because the Chinese shampoo client, a man who unwittingly went about introducing himself as the 'Head of Hair', had signed off on a campaign. On this occasion, however, Chen was not in a party mood and I found him sulking in a corner, perhaps, I thought, because Li had once again turned down his advances.

During the course of the evening we talked about a wide range of subjects, from English Premier League football (of which he was an avid fan) to the vagaries of the weather, until he brought up the subject of the Long March. Chen told his version of the story, mentioning how children could not go on the march, and how Mao had left his own son behind in a place called Yudu.

'They say he was never seen or heard from again,' said Chen.

If Mao An Hong were still alive, I thought, he would be in his late seventies now. I pictured a doting father, possibly even a grandfather, with skin like brown leather and a weathered straw hat perched on his balding head, leaning on a hoe in the walled garden of his mud-brick home as he surveyed a neat row of cabbages. This man, would he even know who he was? Would he even suspect he was the last surviving son of the 'Great Helmsman', whose ideals had formed a nation but also led to the agonising deaths of countless millions of his countrymen?

Chen shook his head slowly. 'But I don't believe that is the end of it.'

I asked Chen what he meant by this statement. He looked me in the eye, swilling the whisky around in his glass.

'If I told you, you would not believe me,' he said finally.

'Try me,' I replied.

Despite my best efforts, however, Chen could not be persuaded to divulge anything further on the subject. Just then, also, the lovely Li had found a table top upon which she could dance, as was her wont, and for the moment, all the men in the room — Chen, half a dozen drunken ex-pats, a handful of Thai staff and me — were under her spell.

* * *

Over the following weeks I was to hear more snippets relating to Chen's background, and not always from Chen himself. Li was equally interested when I broached the subject of Mao's lost son with her in the office, and she began quizzing Chen too. No doubt her questions were met with more enthusiastic responses from the lovesick businessman than mine. In a way, Li became my mole, passing on information that Chen would possibly have preferred to keep to himself and certainly not made available to a prying foreigner. Most of it was of little interest, but, on my last night in Bangkok, all that changed.

With my contract over and the project completed, I retired with a few other senior agency staff, a mix of creatives and suits, to a local bar in the red-light district of Patpong. Evan was Welsh and had been in Bangkok long enough to know its seedy nightlife pretty well. Terry was English and probably the least comfortable in the surrounds we now found ourselves in. Chopper, a big Australian, had the foulest mouth on anyone I had ever encountered. Though, in saying that, Chopper could carry it off well: angels would blush when he spoke, but they would still lean in closer to hear what he had to say.

'Fuck off Taff, the Chop's getting the beers,' he boomed when we entered the bar. Evan put his money away and Chopper disappeared into the crowd, elbowing his way through to the sole bartender. He returned a few minutes later clutching four pints of Guinness.

'Blow me! Are you pricks blind? Do you see who's up on the stage dancing?'

In one movement we all turned our heads to the back of the bar where a flickering strobe light was illuminating the lithe frame of a topless dancer. Her white bikini briefs shone out against her dark skin as she swayed in time to the hypnotic rhythm of the music, and her long, straight hair cascaded down her slender shoulders and pert bosom. It was hard to see her clearly, but I soon recognised her from the way she moved, even before I saw her face.

'It's bloody Li,' yelled Chopper.

It was no great surprise in Bangkok to see one of your Thai workmates trying to earn a few extra baht. Wages weren't great for the locals and Li's position within the company was not a senior one. A second job was almost a necessity.

'She's amazing,' murmured Evan.

'Amazing,' echoed Terry.

Chopper took a large gulp of beer and wiped his mouth with the back of his hand.

'And nice melons to boot,' he added, before waving at Li to catch her attention. We watched as Li smiled and waved back, then mimed downing an imaginary glass of whisky in one shot before casually tossing the glass over her shoulder, all in time with the music.

'Amazing,' repeated Terry wistfully.

'Better get her ladyship a JD on the rocks, guys,' said Chopper, heading back to the bar. 'Looks like she's coming over.'

Sure enough, Li had left the stage and was pulling a white T-shirt over her head as she walked through the busy throng of drinkers, drawing admiring glances from almost all of them. Just then, the door to the pub opened behind us and a blast of hot air roared in off the street, before being beaten back by the air conditioning. One thing that wasn't going to be beaten back, however, was Chopper's wife, a blonde-haired pocket-battleship of a woman in baggy grey track pants, slippers and a T-shirt, the attire normally reserved for evenings in front of the TV at home. She strode in and surveyed the room disapprovingly, spotting our table within seconds.

'Hi boys, seen that useless husband of mine?'

We all looked at each other, feigning ignorance a little too enthusiastically. I noticed Li had also changed tack and was now over by the cigarette machine. Chopper meanwhile was still buried in the crowd.

'Well if you see him tell him to get his arse home pronto,' she said, quietly taking in the fact that there were four glasses at the table and only three of us. 'And you, Terry. I thought you had a new girlfriend at home.'

'I was just going actually,' said Terry defensively, sweeping his car keys and cigarette lighter off the table.

Suddenly Evan knocked back his drink. 'Mind if I get a lift, mate?' he asked, no doubt fearful that Chopper's wife would soon be on the phone to his own partner back at his apartment.

'Sure,' replied Terry, throwing a cursory glance in my direction at the same time. I was in no hurry though, and declined the invitation to join them. They left minutes later with the pocket-battleship at the fore, her wake dragging them both out into the heady warmth of the Bangkok night.

Chopper then reappeared and, as if by delayed reaction, suddenly seemed to realise he should be elsewhere. He deposited Li's drink on the table and, with barely a word, headed out the door and into a waiting cab. With luck he'd beat his wife home.

I looked towards the dispenser and saw Li was wandering over, a pack of cigarettes in one hand. She sat up on one of the high stools at the table and held up the whisky glass.

'Did you hear Chen has asked me to marry him?'

'Wow, that was fast,' I replied.

She offered me a cigarette. I said no but lit hers.

'Do you think I should say yes?' she asked.

I nodded. 'Maybe. But wouldn't you be more interested if it was his sister who was asking?'

Again came the sexy grin. It was automatic with Li. She just had a smile that gladdened the hearts of men. How cruel God could be sometimes, to confer such a gift upon someone who had no use for it.

'You know he's been telling me quite a lot about his family.'

I leant in a little closer as she stirred her drink with a straw then raised it to her lips.

'I think you might be interested.'

What Li had to say was fascinating. Chen was from a village in Jiangxi province, near a town called Ganzhou, where the Communist Party had first taken root in the late 1920s. Early on, his parents were actively involved in recruiting for the Party, something they had progressively less trouble doing, as the peasants were growing increasingly dissatisfied with their treatment by landowners. However, the landowners got wind of Chen's parents' activities and forced them from their home, sending them permanently into exile. That was how they had come to Thailand.

Nevertheless, they kept up a regular correspondence with the Party chairman in that region, a man known simply as Xiao, and, over the years, learnt of the gradual rise of Mao Tse-tung through the Party ranks. Xiao became a loyal follower of Mao and, some said, a confidant. He knew things that even those higher up in the Party may not have been aware of, such was the closeness of the relationship.

Of course Mao was not universally loved in political circles. Feared was probably closer to the truth, for Mao was known for a sudden and irrational temper that could spell doom for anyone unlucky enough to be caught up in it. Purges within the Party were common, and often senseless in their brutality. His treatment of local tribal leaders was unforgiving at times also. That brought Mao more enemies than friends — enemies who waited patiently for the moment when they could attack him. Indeed, in 1930 Mao's second wife, Yang Kahui, and her son Mao Anying were captured by a local warlord and handed on a plate to the Nationalist forces of Chiang Kai-shek, who wanted her to publicly renounce Mao and the Communists. Despite being tortured, she refused and was therefore executed by firing squad, watched by her son. Later, He Zizhen narrowly avoided capture and possibly a similar fate. But by then Mao was wise to the threat and took the necessary measures to protect her.

According to what Li had learnt from Chen, when the Long March began in Yudu and Mao and He Zizhen were forced to leave Mao An Hong behind, it was Xiao who took charge. He arranged for the boy to be entrusted to Mao's younger brother, Mao Zetan, who secretly hid the child for safe keeping, without telling anyone where. However, in the months of fighting that followed, Mao Zetan was killed by the Nationalists. All knowledge of the boy's whereabouts then appeared to be lost.

'So what do you think happened to him?' I asked.

An older woman had seen us and was walking over. It was the mama-san, the owner of the bar and the one who 'ran' the girls.

Li answered in a slightly lower voice. 'One thing I do know. In China, people don't move far from their local villages. So if he is still alive, he'll probably be in the same area of Yudu that Mao Zetan hid him in.'

The mama-san stopped beside Li and stroked her dark hair, smiling at me. Li on the other hand wasn't smiling.

'You like?' she asked in a shrill voice.

'Come on,' I said to Li. 'Let's go somewhere else.'

I got down off my stool but Li hadn't moved. She was looking down at the table, tracing a finger through the ring of condensation left behind by her empty glass.

'I can't,' she said. 'I can't go until someone pays my bar fine.'

'Five hundred baht,' squealed the mama-san expectantly. She had come round to my side and was holding out a chubby hand. It wasn't a lot of money. I fumbled in my wallet for the notes and paid for Li's freedom. As we left I saw the mama-san laughing, hands on hips, thrusting her pelvis in and out.

Outside in the humid streets of Patpong, Bangkok's infamous red-light district was still humming with people and traffic. I looked at my watch — it was 2 a.m. We'd been talking for hours. I felt a bead of sweat run down my back.

'What now?' she asked.

'I'm getting you a taxi home, that's what.'

A cab arrived in seconds and as she jumped in I gave her a few hundred baht. It was a small amount, nothing compared to what she would have earned if I'd been taking her home.

'For the taxi fare,' I said.

She nodded sweetly. 'Good luck finding the boy. You'll need it. In Jiangxi alone there are nearly 50 million people.'

A quarter of all humankind calls China home. The thought of finding any one person, or even a group of people was mindboggling. Added to that was the fact that any trail leading to Little Mao was almost 80 years old. Chen's story was a start, but somehow I doubted its reliability. It could be true, but in all honesty I just didn't know. The official version said little when it came to Mao An Hong: 'Whereabouts unknown. No further information available'. It was quite possibly the greatest and most frustrating full stop in history. The only way to even get close to finding out was to return to China, to the places where Little Mao had last been seen. And that's what I decided to do. With my contract finished, I was a free man, with time on my side.

'And hey,' came Li's voice from inside the cab.

I bent down and looked in through the open window.

'Thanks,' she said happily, still clutching the money. 'I owe you one.'

As the cab pulled away she smiled her devastating smile and winked mischievously.

'No Li', I thought, watching the taillights disappear around the next corner, 'I definitely owe you.'

THREE

THE CHINESE WERE PRACTISING FOR THE ARRIVAL OF THEIR Olympic guests by behaving in a thoroughly Western fashion: the queues for tickets within the cement-and-marble interior of Shanghai's main train station were long and orderly. But only up to a certain point. All pretences of decorum and social civility were thrown out when it mattered most: at the ticket window. From that moment on, it was a return to the age-old Oriental custom of pushing and shoving.

Window Seven was no different. A short distance ahead of me in the queue, as many as three to four people were trying to squeeze in front of the glass partition that separated them from the glum-faced girl selling tickets. She dealt with each and every one of them in a way that underlined her position of superiority, and their inferiority. One impolite word from anyone wanting a ticket risked a cold shoulder and a return to the back of the line, so while they elbowed each other and struggled to get some part of their body in front of her, they were desperately trying to be nice to her too.

Twenty metres back, in a relative oasis of calm, I surveyed the giant map of China that hung on the wall above all the ticket windows. Convention and logic suggested that one should begin looking for someone where they were last seen. Indeed it might be unnecessary to go any further than this geographical bull's-eye. In this case, that would be near the town of Yudu in Jiangxi province, to the southwest of where I presently stood. However, I had decided to throw convention out the window. I would begin the journey at the end, so to speak. The Long March had finished near the provinces of Gansu and Shaanxi to the northwest, on the edge of the Gobi Desert. By beginning my journey there and following the march in reverse, I would give myself time to acclimatise to the altitude, improve my rusty Mandarin and hopefully meet up with some interesting people along the way. The only question was which town to travel to first.

Quite surprisingly, however, that decision was made for me by a most unlikely candidate: a 210-centimetre-tall Chinese basketball player named Shenzhen Liu.

I reached the window in due course and stuck an arm through the gap beneath the glass partition. In my hand I held out a couple of red 100-yuan notes. Unfortunately, my arm wasn't the only one competing for the attention of the disinterested ticket seller. Many others waved fistfuls of cash frantically in front of her face, accompanied by pleading voices asking a myriad of questions. My own voice was drowned out; besides, she had already seen me and decided I looked too much like hard work. It was just then that a shadow was cast over the increasingly frenetic transactions. The ticket seller stopped taking money, the jabbering of voices quietened to a murmur and the swarm of hopeful travellers craned their necks skywards in hushed awe.

He was huge. So much so that the top of his red tracksuit trousers soared well past the level of the counter. The rest of him, which was adorned in a red jacket with white stripes on the sleeves, rose up to a height that made the ceiling appear lower. His face was wide and brown, with the high cheekbones of someone with Mongol ancestry, and bore an expression that was somewhat impassive, as if the commotion he was now causing was something he was not entirely easy with. He reached down and slid some money under the glass partition because his hand was too big to fit through, and in a deep voice requested a ticket. By now everyone had stood back to give him room — all except for one. I still had my arm under the glass and it was this that drew his attention. He eyed the money between my fingers, took in my jeans and old walking boots, the worn khaki shoulder bag at my feet and, most probably, the slight look of exasperation in my eyes, then spoke a few words of broken English that would eventually prove to be more than significant.

'Can I help?' he asked.

With a nod I explained how I was trying to find out what time the next train was leaving for the northwest. He spoke briefly with the ticket seller then turned back to me.

'You wish to go today?'

'If possible,' I replied.

He then looked at his own ticket, which seemed so small in his hand, and pointed a long finger at the line of Chinese characters at the top.

'This is a hard-sleeper ticket to Xining, leaving in two hours. One way.'

Xining is the provincial capital of Qinghai province, a highland town of over a million people perched on the edge of the Tibetan plateau, and a major jumping-off point on the northwestern rail line. I'd been there once before, years ago, and from memory it was brown, dusty and had no great claim to fame, other than being within easy reach of a number of key Tibetan monasteries and historical sites. As far as starting points went, however, it was at least in the same locale as Gansu and Shaanxi provinces, Mao's strongholds at the end of the Long March. And I had a hunch that the journey there was going to be more than just a train ride; indeed, something was telling me this was all part of a grander plan, as if fate was steering me in this direction for good reason.

I leant towards the glass partition and, in my best Mandarin, requested an identical train ticket.

'You don't want to go soft-sleeper?' the giant asked, with sudden concern.

I told him soft-sleeper was for the rich tourist and, besides, if hard-sleeper was good enough for him it was good enough for me. The ticket seller duly printed out the ticket and slid it under the glass. All the time, however, she never once took her eyes off the giant. Maybe it was because he was so tall, or maybe it was because for the first time he was smiling happily, with a grin so great it could have lit up a darkened room.

'Then we go together. My name is Liu,' he announced proudly, holding out his hand. 'But you can call me Mr Golden.'

I reached up and shook his hand.

'Nice to meet you Mr Golden.'

FOUR

Train K376 for Xining was full when it departed from Platform 5 that afternoon, with almost all the passengers of Carriage Fourteen and some from the adjoining carriages gathered outside our compartment. The lure of the giant and the foreigner was too much to resist.

The gathering had begun with one or two fellow passengers walking the length of the corridor and pausing outside our compartment for longer than was necessary to look out the window. They would eventually amble off, only to return with friends or relatives eager to witness Liu for themselves. It wasn't long before someone broke the ice with the first question. From that moment on, the inquisition started. Where were we from? How tall was Liu? How tall was I?

The compartments in hard-sleeper are made up of six bunks, three on each side, all of which are open to the corridor, so there is nowhere to hide. From all directions faces strained for a better view, including one little guy who had climbed into the luggage rack. Liu was sitting hunched over on the bottom bunk, his knees protruding into the air like twin Everests, while I was stretched out in the middle bunk directly opposite. Most of the questions were aimed at him, so I was able to relax, but I couldn't help but feel a sense of pity. No doubt this was the play enacted on every stage he ventured upon. Chinese people are naturally inquisitive and have no qualms about intruding: in a country of so many, there is no room for personal space. So Liu faced a barrage of questions until the attendant in charge of the carriage, a stout woman who wore a badge pinned to her chest printed with the number 007, snapped at everyone to return to their beds so that she could check our tickets. It was a welcome respite, even if it would prove only short.

When she had gone, I looked down to see Liu lying on his side with his face to the wall. He had his legs bent, but his feet still stuck a long way out into the hallway. He was already asleep, or perhaps he was feigning it to escape the crowds. Either way I left him in peace and watched through the window as the green rice fields of Anhui province eventually replaced Shanghai's urban sprawl. Here and there, small railside villages flashed by, their inhabitants busy in the surrounding fields, backs bent to the task of producing rice for a nation. It was obvious that every inch of ground had been planted with something edible. The roof of one house boasted a harvest of corn ready for picking. Atop another was a tiny allotment of squash. Nothing was wasted, even the light: only when the last rays of the sun had set did the farmers return to their homes.

Anhui had been one of the provinces worst affected by the floods that brought so much despair to the region in the mid-2000s. Millions of people had been made homeless and hundreds of thousands of houses had been destroyed when the Huaihe

River burst its banks after three days of constant downpours. Some three-storey buildings were entirely submerged.

It's almost impossible for foreigners to fathom the scale of natural disasters in China, to grasp the human, material and financial damage catastrophic events can inflict when the number of people involved is so great. In a single disaster, thousands can perish, millions may be displaced and billions of dollars are often required to make even the most basic repairs. Even now, several months on from what the local authorities called the worst flood in 50 years, the evidence of its impact on Anhui lay just outside the window. Moments before the sun dipped below the distant mountain ranges, I caught sight of a man on the doorstep of his wooden home, fishing for his evening meal in the expanse of water that surrounded him.

* * *

It was dark when 007 came down the passageway, banging a metal trolley laden with food and drink against the iron bunk heads. Pot noodles were the main course, with a side of lukewarm rice and skewered meat if you were game enough to try. I opted for the noodles, sprinkled on the various powders and sauces that came with it and then went to the hot-water tap in the next carriage to fill up the pot. A sign attached to the metal cylinder warned me:

Dangerous section. Pay your attention.

Somewhat unwisely, perhaps because I was having a quiet chuckle to myself at the errant translation, I failed to heed the

A man delivers coal bricks in Gansu Province

instruction and scalded myself when the incredibly hot water splashed over my hand. Nursing the injury and a full pot of cooking noodles, I went back to one of the fold-down seats by the windows that lined the passageway. It was then I noticed the elderly man sitting in another seat a few metres further on. As I poured a little cold water from my water bottle onto the burn, he smiled and nodded in sympathy. Then he raised his arms, showing that one of his hands was missing. A leathery stump stuck out from his navy blue jacket and looked like a small, tightly clenched fist. In his other, good hand he held a tiny wicker cage, from which came a soft chirruping sound. The old man pointed at the cage with his stump and, through tobacco-stained teeth, cheerfully said: 'Cu zhi, cu zhi.'

I had no idea what he was saying, but it didn't take a genius to work out that he was referring to his pet cricket. For 2,000 years crickets have had a special place in Chinese culture. They've long been prized by farmers, who say they can read the change in the seasons based on the insects' behaviour. Emperors kept them for the beauty of their song and also for their fighting ability, although an imperial cricket was more used to living in a cage of gold rather than bamboo. As a boy in Australia I'd made pets of blue-tongue lizards, grass snakes and even a funnel-web spider once, which lived only a short while before meeting an untimely end under the weight of my father's shovel. But never had I befriended a cricket.

The old man got up from his seat and came over to perch at the end of one of the bunks. Again he stabbed at the cage with his handless wrist and repeated the words 'Cu zhi,' much to the growing amusement of the other passengers who were watching. Then he pointed outside the windows before pulling an imaginary blanket round himself and shivering.

A deep voice sounded from the corridor behind me.

'It is an old Chinese expression.'

It was Liu, stirring his own pot of noodles and standing with his head ducked down so that he wouldn't hit it against the overhead luggage rack.

'*Cu zhi* means to start making clothes for winter,' he continued. 'The cricket makes this sound in autumn, warning people to get ready for the cold.'

I was amazed. Not just at this interesting piece of local folklore, but also at the way Liu was now speaking English. I told him this and he shrugged his wide shoulders.

'My English is very bad, but since we met I've started to remember my lessons.'

As it turned out, my gargantuan travelling companion was just the kind of person I would ideally choose to spend my first days in China with. As the kilometres passed beneath us, we were each able to gain answers to all kinds of questions. Mine were to do with conditions in Xining, which he had travelled to on several occasions; his were regarding peculiar English sayings, for which he clearly had a penchant.

'What is it when I say, "Bob's your Uncle"?,' he asked at one stage. 'Is this disrespectful to a person's family?'

Happily, I explained that that was unlikely to be the case and that he could use the expression freely to suggest something was going to be fine and dandy.

'Dandy?' he quizzed.

'Dandy also means something is good,' I replied.

He beamed with delight at this new-found knowledge and rolled the words silently round his tongue. Liu was clearly interested in practising and improving his English. The reason, however, wasn't clear until later that evening when we were turning in for bed. He was reaching up to take his suitcase down when the lock broke and sent most of his possessions flying. Apart from a few clothes and a toothbrush, his bag was filled with red Chinese basketballs, airless and flat-packed, by the dozen. Slightly embarrassed, he scooped them up and stuffed them back into his case, but not before the interest of every other passenger was kindled. For the next half an hour they questioned him, as I listened, trying to catch on to the conversation. Most of it was beyond my comprehension, but I did make out one thing that was repeated over and over: the name 'Yao Ming'. I knew he was the famous 230-centimetre Chinese basketball player who had turned pro with the Houston Rockets, a top NBA team in America, and was now China's great hope to lead the national side to a gold medal at the Olympics. I was intrigued to know if Liu was an exponent of the game — he certainly had the physique, after all. Eventually I got the answer, after the pestering subsided and I was able to ask a few questions of my own.

'Mr Golden' had been his court name when he played the game at provincial level; indeed, it sounded as though greater glory would have been his had it not been for an injury that curtailed his playing career. Now he was setting his sights on selling locally made basketballs to offshore markets — hence the need for English — although this, he said, was a long-term business plan. At the same time he would continue promoting the game in the northern and western regions, where the average height of the population was a good deal taller than in the south.

'The tallest man in the world was from Inner Mongolia,' he said slightly wistfully, as the lights dimmed, warning us that we would soon be plunged into darkness for the night. 'He was from Chifeng Shi, where my father comes from.'

'And is your father as tall as you?' I enquired.

'Taller,' came the reply. 'Like a mountain.'

* * *

In the morning I woke to the sound of a cricket chirruping and the slightly distant thud of a ball bouncing on concrete. Gone was the rhythmic clatter of train on track and when I opened my eyes I could see why. We were at a small station and, through the chintz curtains, I saw Liu on the platform teaching the old man with the missing hand how to bounce a basketball. Further down the platform I could see a few others exercising in their own way, mostly the elderly rather than the young, stretching and twisting vigorously to an inaudible beat. They slapped their shoulders to encourage blood flow, while Liu urged his new pupil to shoot for goal. He stood tall and held out his arms, the fingertips of his left hand touching those of his right to form an impromptu hoop. Unfortunately the old man's shot went wide of Liu's outstretched hands and bounced under the train. To make matters worse, the whistle sounded for the train to depart and the guards began shouting and urging the passengers to climb on board. Our own carriage attendant, the fearsome 007, blew her whistle loudly. There was no way Liu could fit under the train to rescue the ball and certainly the old man looked like the task was beyond him. However, with an agility that belied his years, that is exactly what he did. In an instant he was under the carriage and back up on the platform holding the ball in his good hand and smiling broadly.

As the train began to move away, Liu and the ever-belligerent 007 stepped on board, but the old man remained on the platform and waved. It was then I noticed the small, neat bundle of belongings in a faded red-, white- and blue-striped bag, placed on the platform not far from where he stood. No doubt everything he owned was in there — the worldly possessions of a one-handed man. All except for one small thing, however. From his tiny straw enclosure the wee fellow announced his presence with a resounding *chirrup*: next to my pillow was the cricket.

It was a gift, Liu said later. This cricket had apparently won many matches at Shanghai's Ti Lan Qiao cricket markets and earned a small sum of money for its elderly owner. On closer inspection I could see one of its legs hung at a peculiar angle and I assumed this was why the old man had given up such a valuable champion. But no sooner had this thought occurred to me than my new-found friend straightened out his leg and began to look every bit the fearsome fighter of his reputation. Maybe it was my imagination, but I had the distinct impression that the wounded warrior look had been a bit of a ruse.

'What will you call him?' asked Liu.

I thought about this for a moment as the food trolley banged its way past the end of my bunk, pushed malevolently by our surly hostess.

'Bond,' I replied suddenly. 'James Bond.'

Liu looked at me strangely, no doubt thinking this was the worst ever name for a fighting cricket, but the moniker stuck and certainly my cricket didn't mind. He was off on a new adventure, one that would see him vanquish new foes; crush, overcome and annihilate without mercy; lay waste to all contestants; and go down in history as the greatest, most supreme fighting insect of all time.

Or at least something to that effect.

FIVE

Through the mist-shrouded mountains of Shaanxi province we journeyed, the region where the Long March had ended and where Mao had created a Communist stronghold. But in my case, fate and a rather lofty basketball player were taking me further west, past the multi-terraced hillsides of Gansu and, finally, up, up and up to where the red-earth cliffs of Qinghai are split by the muddy Huang Shui, one of the main tributaries of the famous Yellow River.

From the eastern seaboard at Shanghai, you travel 2,200 kilometres to reach Xining and climb an almost equal number of metres in altitude. As Liu had promised, it was fine and cold the morning we arrived at the station, but not freezing. The air was thin, however, and my breathing rate was faintly heavier than normal, a product of Xining's location at the foot of the Tibetan plateau — that vast area commonly referred to as the Roof of the World. Later there would be challenges far greater than this in terms of oxygen deprivation, including mountain passes as high as 4,700 metres, so I thought I should stay long enough in Xining for my body to start acclimatising to high altitude.

Liu was adamant that he would be my guide and so, together, with my fighting cricket in his bamboo cage tucked inside a side pocket of my shoulder bag, we negotiated our way through the terminal and out onto the busy streets of the town. No matter where you go in China, you'll usually find almost every form of transport available outside a train station, and Xining was no different. The buses may have been ancient but they were neatly parked in three rows, each one servicing a different direction. For one yuan you could go a long way, but Liu was unhappy with the quality of the vehicles, so he waved down a passing taxi. He squeezed in the back and I sat beside him, albeit with a lot more ease. The ceiling of the cab had been torn out and replaced by a deep blue lining dotted with stars. Orion's belt hung over our heads and I reached up to touch Bellatrix, one of its brightest stars. Visible from almost anywhere in the world, this was the constellation I looked for each night when I was deep in the mountains of Afghanistan. With many hundreds of kilometres left to walk before I could reach the relative safety of Pakistan, I would gaze upon it before finding a rock to sleep under, drawing strength from something familiar in a strange land.

'I like stars too,' said Liu uncomfortably, with his shins pressed hard against the front seat. 'But in the sky, not in this shitty taxi.'

We drove along a wide and dusty road. The traffic lanes were indiscernible, so the horn was used at regular intervals to let people know we were coming. Carts pulled by donkeys were given particularly loud warnings, presumably because they might change direction at short notice, which they then invariably did, although this may have been a result of our passing so close and at such speed. Pedestrians were also made to think twice about trying to cross the road in front of us, and it was only the foolhardy or desperate that attempted to do so. Despite all this, we got to the town centre in just under a few minutes, still in one piece and all for just a few cents.

Liu pointed out a hotel down a narrow passageway where I could stay. But, first of all, he announced, we would go and see his business partner, who lived in a small apartment a few blocks away.

'He collects hubcaps,' he said in a matter-of-fact way.

'From cars?' I asked.

'Of course. Where would you collect them from in your country?'

'Cars, I suppose,' I replied.

Liu nodded sagely, and then after a while said, 'You see, our countries are very much the same.'

Just then a bright yellow rubbish truck drove by, with the tune of 'Good King Wenceslas' blaring from a megaphone tied to its bonnet.

'Yep,' I said quietly. 'Just like home.'

* * *

The first-floor apartment, in a large multistorey residential complex of rotting concrete, was a single room with a freezer and free-standing air-con unit in one corner, next to a rather ornate goldfish bowl filled with live turtles. Sitting in a large leather sofa watching the television and wearing the traditional embroidered-silk clothes of a Manchurian was an extremely old man. An ancient white moustache hung down in two strands on either side of his mouth, making him look like the classic Western image of an elderly Kung Fu master. He was 90 years old but looked over 100, and was Liu's partner's grandfather, Song Yu.

Liu's business partner had greeted us warmly and was not surprised to see me — Liu had already phoned and told him we were coming. Song Jr was in his early thirties and wore his hair close cropped in a military style. He was half the size of Liu, which made them quite the odd couple, though what Song Jr lacked in height he made up for in enthusiasm. He was clearly the businessman in the partnership and his cellphone rang every few minutes as testimony to the fact. The old man paid no notice and invited us to sit in two leather chairs opposite him. With a croaky voice he ordered Song Jr's daughter, a sweet girl still short of her teens, to bring bitter tea. Soon she brought out a steaming ceramic pot with a bamboo handle and four glasses. We sat in silence as the tea was poured, with the old man being the last to be served. After the first sip, the conversation started, with Liu acting as interpreter.

Song Yu was of huge interest to me because he was old enough to remember the Long March. Broaching the subject wasn't easy, however. There were political hurdles and sensitivities to get around — for example, had he been for or against the Communists? Did he remember Mao as a great leader or a great mistake?

I decided to begin by asking more general questions relating to the time when Song Yu was growing up, a period of significant conflict. It transpired that he had fought against the Japanese in 1937. At that time the Japanese Empire was eager to seize land in all directions, most notably from its nearest neighbour, China, which it regarded as hugely inferior. Japan's naval stranglehold on the China Sea allowed it to invade Shanghai, the perfect port from which to expand further and achieve the empire's ultimate goal, total control of the Asia–Pacific region. It was men like Song Yu who had stalled and eventually blocked them, preventing a complete military victory over China that might have had significant consequences in the Second World War. Had Japan enjoyed unbridled access to China's rich natural resources, it could have become an even more powerful force, and then who knows what might have happened? Was this old man, and the many others like him, the real reason we speak English in Australia and New Zealand today, and not Japanese?

I felt guilty probing for more information because it was clear that revisiting this period was painful for him, and that his memories were deeply buried. The Japanese forces had been brutal, while the Chinese side had fought with equal ferocity. The nearly four-month-long battle for Shanghai was later referred to as China's own version of Stalingrad, due to its intense house-to-house fighting. Although eventually overrun by the Japanese and driven all the way back beyond Nanking, the Chinese fighters had given the army of the Rising Sun a bloody nose. Before the invasion of Shanghai, the Japanese had perceived themselves as being like gods compared to their inferior Chinese combatants. Now, having been made to fight tooth and nail for every square metre of the city, they were humbled. They never really recovered their sense of cultural and military superiority and were something of a damaged lot afterwards, never again coming close to achieving the complete dominion over China they had once envisaged.

We chatted politely about his time working in a bank and how he had subsequently moved to Xining to be close to his son, who worked in telecommunications, a burgeoning industry in this far-flung region, ironically selling, amongst other things, the latest cellular telephone technology from Japan.

The talk was all very discreet, which made the revelation from Song Yu's little great-granddaughter all the more surprising when it came. She had been sitting beside her great-grandfather all along, listening attentively to both the English and Chinese conversations. Then, without warning, she did what little girls do best when they're super proud of their relations: she began to boast.

'My great-grandfather was a brave soldier,' she said with gleeful naivety, 'who fought against the Japanese *and* the Communists.'

The old man did not bother to listen to the English being spoken. He sat still, sipping his tea and watching a news item on the television.

'But Chairman Mao was too strong and my great-grandfather's army was defeated near Yan'an.'

I resisted the temptation to interrupt, in case it stopped her in her tracks. Sure enough, she kept going.

'Of course, he realised that Chairman Mao was a good and wise leader and, with many other soldiers, joined him to help create our great and free nation.'

She sat back as pleased as punch with this recitation of China's history and her family's role in it. No doubt it was a sanitised version of events, repeated word for word from her schoolbooks, and quite possibly given to her by Song Jr in an attempt to explain his grandfather's early political leanings. One thing was sure, however: Grandfather Song had been on the side of the Nationalists under 'Generalissimo' Chiang Kai-shek, and was possibly even amongst those who had hounded the Long Marchers along their route. In others words, he had been the enemy. The big question was, had he really seen the error of his ways and joined Mao voluntarily, or was this now-frail and elderly gent still a dissenting voice?

The man himself was never going to answer that, however. The news had ended and he was engrossed in a game show in which two teams were being challenged to make an incredibly complex ferris wheel out of chopsticks and cardboard tubing. A 'blue team' of university students was competing against a 'red team' of soldiers and there was a lot of shouting and gesticulating by their two pushy female leaders. In the end, the red team triumphed: the army was victorious over the intelligentsia. It was the Communist Revolution all over again, on prime-time afternoon television.

We left after the last drop of tea had been drunk and eventually made our way to the hotel Liu had recommended in the centre of town. It was very cheap but clean and was located in a backstreet, with no apparent sign alluding to its presence, as far as I could tell. It was the kind of place I probably would not have been allowed to stay at if I hadn't been with Liu. There were bigger, more expensive hotels for foreigners and the local police were often adamant that Western travellers stayed at these places — 'for their own security', they said.

But luxury and glamour always come at a price, and not just a monetary cost. The big hotels make you feel separate from the local people and their day-to-day activities, whereas in the small, sometimes rundown inns and hostels you often find yourself side by side with them. From experience I knew this was the best way to garner the kind of information I would require to ensure the success of my mission. If I were to discover anything about the missing boy, it would almost certainly come from meeting and talking with as many ordinary Chinese people as possible. The language was still a problem, but I had had one idea on how to deal with this while talking with Liu on the train. At my request he had selected a fresh page in my spare journal and written, in Mandarin, an explanation of who I was and what I was doing in China. This letter of introduction ended with a request for the reader, whoever it might be, to add what they knew of the boy in their own words — anonymously if they so wished. At the time I wasn't sure whether it would be of much use, whether people could be persuaded to write anything of consequence. I thought that, at best, it might result in an interesting aside to the main story, a motley collection of ramblings from people I met along the way, which I would then have translated at a later date. In the end, however, it would prove to be something of even greater value than my passport: it would become a key to worlds I could never otherwise have entered.

A roadside hairdresser in Xining

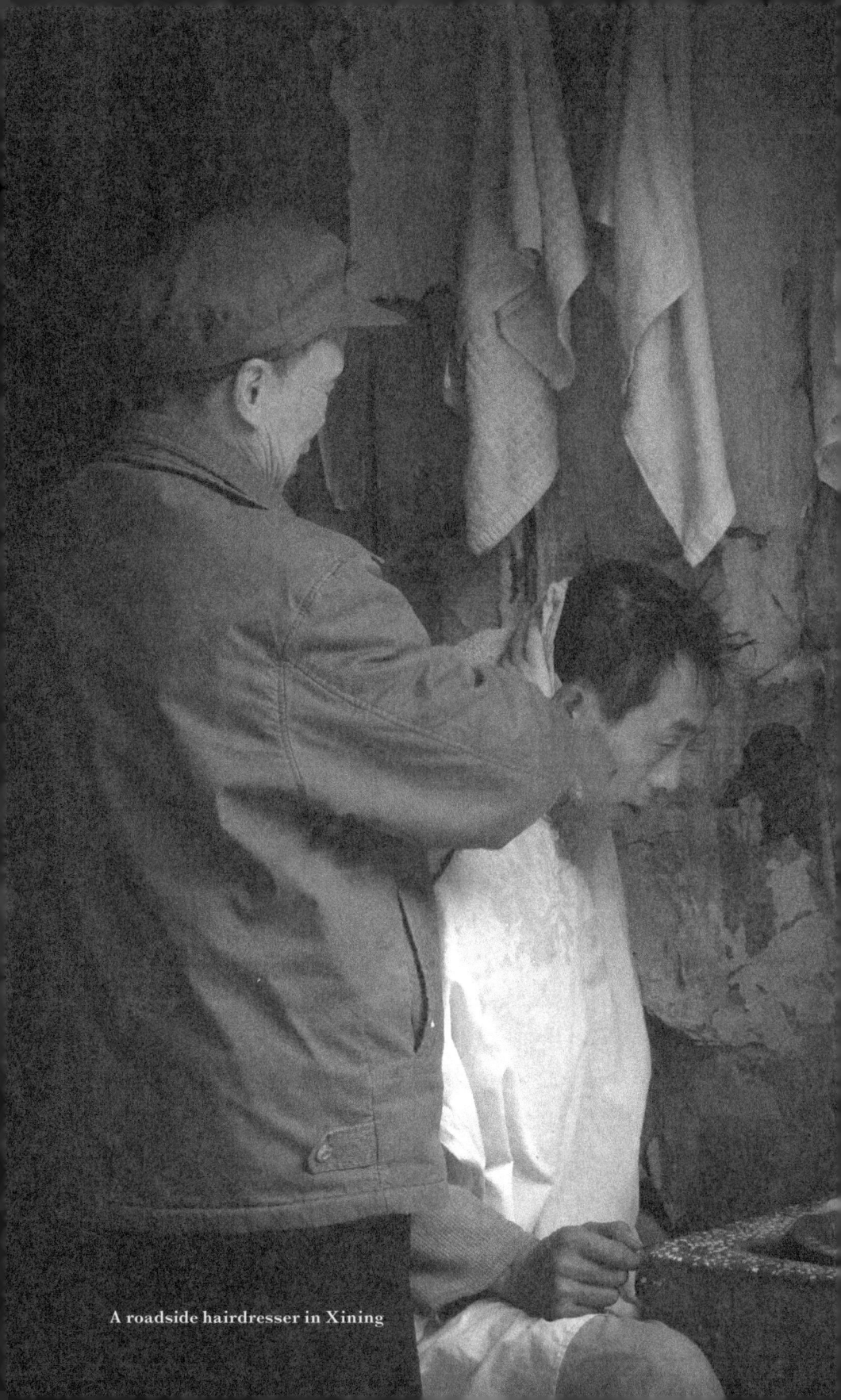

SIX

In the early morning, bare-chested and with no shoes on his feet, the boy was lying in the sun on a bed of recently butchered pigs. At first I thought he was asleep, but when the rickety old cart he was reclining in swerved to avoid a beggar in the street, he opened his eyes and happened to look in my direction. His expression was curious, then dumbfounded, as if I might have been part of his daydream. He shook his head and blinked, before a smile creased his face. The connection between us lasted for a few seconds more, until he and his bloodied cargo bumped and rumbled their way round a corner and disappeared.

I was near the bus station, having bought a ticket that would take me south, over the ranges and up onto the grasslands of the Tibetan plateau in a few days' time. Keeping to my plan, I intended to roughly follow the route of the Long March, except in reverse. Like the fabled Silk Road, there was no path as such. Those men and women who had made this journey long ago had taken many different trails, sometimes separated by hundreds of kilometres, so it was a more general route that I would try to emulate. Actually it wasn't so much a plan either, more a statement of intent, a loose arrangement with time and fate, designed to allow me to just drift and see what, or more importantly who, I might run into. My intention was to journey south towards the small, mostly Tibetan villages of Maduo then Yushu, before turning east and tackling the mountainous region separating Qinghai from Sichuan before the snows came. It would then be a case of tracking further east towards one of the known starting points of the Long March, an area called Yudu, also the place where Little Mao had last been seen.

For the time being, however, I wanted to get used to the altitude and have a look around Xining. My giant friend was already plying his wares at the local schools, no doubt causing quite a stir with his massive frame, all the while looking out for long-legged athletes he could recruit to play professionally. We had arranged to catch up later that evening, so I was on my own again and preferring it that way for the moment.

By the river, which was wide and shallow through lack of rain, I came across an outdoor pool hall in the shade of some willow trees. There were a dozen or so very well worn tables, about half of which were being used by a large group of young men. Most were Han Chinese, while the minority were Tibetan. The Tibetans wore felt cowboy hats, black leather boots and thick sheepskin coats of a type known as the *chuba*. The wool was on the inside and the sleeves were so long that they reached down to the ground. Normally on warm days the right arm and shoulder were exposed, helping to regulate the body's temperature, but today these boys meant business. Their coats were undone completely and hung down from the waist like skirts, revealing white cotton undershirts that gleamed brightly in the morning sun.

It was the Tibetans who invited me over to watch their best player battle a Han Chinese boy in what was some kind of final. I was told by one young lad that their hero had never lost a single game and he certainly had the swagger of a champion. The relatively clean-cut Chinese boy, in his light blue T-shirt and jeans, looked quite nervous in comparison to his competitor, who walked around with his cue slung over one shoulder like a rifle, cigarette hanging from the corner of his mouth. Like many Tibetans, he wore his black hair long and his cheeks were wind-burnt and ruddy. Ethnically, the two boys were far apart. The game, however, was close.

After 20 minutes of play, with only the black ball remaining and the Han Chinese boy looking down his cue at an easy shot to the corner pocket, it seemed the game was over. I felt sure that at any other time he would have nailed that shot, but on this occasion a handful of pretty tough-looking Tibetans were glaring at him across the table. The ball rattled the pocket but stayed up, half a centimetre from the hole, and that was that. The Chinese boy slunk away, as did his compatriots, leaving the Tibetans to strut about victoriously once their champion had slotted the ball neatly into the pocket.

Delighted, they invited me to go with them to an Internet café in an upstairs room just across the road. It seemed that just about every kid in Xining was there, playing computer games. The darkened room was packed — evidence of the new culture pervading the old, which undoubtedly had the bigwigs in Beijing worried. Although, looking around, they probably didn't have any real cause for concern. Rather than being corrupted by Western ideologies and unsanctioned global news sites that might criticise their government, the youth of China were simply plugged into the virtual world of online gaming.

The owner of the café was a Hui Muslim man in his forties who called himself Ma, a common derivative of the name Mohammad. He wore a white skullcap that shone brightly in the single ray of light that he allowed through the black curtains behind him. It was there he said to remind him of the time of day, and therefore the time to go to prayer.

Ma surveyed the room full of computer screens with a dispassionate look.

'My brother owns a restaurant,' he said in halting English. 'I wish I also had a restaurant. The Hui are wonderful at cooking. Our food is the finest in all China. But instead of a restaurant, I have this.' He gestured with his arm towards the room, where row upon row of faces were glued to their screens, fingers working feverishly at the keyboard controls.

'They spend all their time killing each other.'

Sure enough, on every screen was the same fantasy adventure game, featuring martial arts and magic potions, in which, it seemed, it was every man for himself. Now and again, a cry would ring out across the room as another would-be contender was brought down by someone else's blade or the jaws of a mystical creature, only to come to life again seconds later, the only apparent damage being to the young combatant's ego. There were even several groups of young Buddhist monks, in their crimson gowns, each totally engrossed in what was happening on a fellow student's screen. They clapped their hands enthusiastically as one of their group despatched foe after foe, only to then meet an untimely end and be forced to surrender his place at the keyboard to the next challenger.

All around the world it was the same, in every Internet gaming hall and many a living room: death and immediate resurrection, over and over. In this instance, of course, there was an ironic connection with the local religion. Perhaps this was the attraction: the laws of reincarnation were being brought to life in a medium these youngsters had no problem understanding. Rather than books and the endless drone of scripture to teach the basics of Buddhism, here was a more entertaining form of instruction, albeit with a somewhat unhealthy dose of violence thrown in. Quite the opposite of being idle downtime, this was quite possibly a classroom for these young, shaven-headed monks.

I stood behind them unobserved and watched as the melee of frantic button-pushing continued, until one young monk caught on and gave me away. I asked if I could play and, begrudgingly, the boy at the keyboard was made to leave his cherished seat. I was told the game was called *Mèng Huàn X Yóu*, meaning *Fantasy Westward Journey*, but any hope I had of understanding its complexity soon vanished as my sabre-wielding on-screen persona disappeared in a ball of fire. The voices around me groaned in despair. But no sooner had I perished than I was back up again, striding fearlessly into battle — only to meet a similar fate, this time at the end of a blue lightning bolt. That was enough for the boy whose seat I'd taken, and he reached in and started hitting buttons at high speed, invoking several deadly curses and a ball of energy that then laid waste to every living thing on the computer screen. That was it — I was done.

Politely edged out, I resumed the position of onlooker rather than participant.

'They play and play and play for hours. It is good money,' Ma said, rubbing thumb against forefinger, 'but not for me. I do not like all this computer fighting. It is not sport. I prefer crickets.'

My ears pricked up.

'Do you mean fighting crickets?' I asked.

'The finest in all of Qinghai,' he replied. 'You like to watch also?'

It was a silly question of course. Clearly Ma had no idea who he was talking to. Was I not in possession of the greatest fighting cricket of all? The legendary James Bond, master of the most cunning of moves, able to turn defence into offence with a single 'Oh look, I've got a busted leg; no I don't, ha-haa!' — *Chop!*

'Watch?' I replied, with mock disgust. 'I can do better than that.'

* * *

That evening I returned to the Internet café with James merrily chirruping in his bamboo cage. Ma was waiting on the street with his own favoured insects, all in their own separate cages, including a rather regal looking chap, with a black body and brown head, in a Tupperware container. This was, he announced proudly, Li Mu Bai, named after the character played by Chow Yun-fat in his first big movie, *Crouching Tiger, Hidden Dragon.*

I told him I was familiar with the movie, and the actor himself. Ma's eyes bulged in their sockets.

'You know Chow Yun-fat?'

It was bending the truth a little to say I 'knew' the actor, but, as a traveller in China in 1989, I had been invited to play a bit part in a scene in one of his early movies, *God of Gamblers*. The scene was set on Hong Kong harbour, on a passenger liner, and I was one of several background extras in tuxedos. It would be the first and last of my movie appearances; however, I could, to this day, still point to the few seconds of the movie where yours truly lingered, fake cocktail in hand, chatting nonchalantly with a pretty Swedish girl, as Chow Yun-fat walked by, flanked by his entourage of on-screen henchmen.

This was big news with Ma, and when we arrived at the location for the fight, which was a short distance away in a richly cushioned room at the back of his brother's restaurant, I was introduced as 'an actor from Hong Kong'. The group of men who sat on the floor in a circle looked up as one and gawped, then, sensing there was money to be made off the wealthy stranger, shuffled along to allow us both to sit.

At the centre of their circle was a small glass box with a central partition separating two male crickets, whose owners were stroking their antennae with sticks to make them more aggressive. Bets were laid and the money was looked after by Ma's white-aproned brother, who then dished out the winnings while his wife dished out rice and skewered lamb in the restaurant. Cries of 'Eurghh!' filled the room whenever a cricket was defeated, followed by a 'Weiyah!' from the victor. Although it was a blood sport, if a cricket simply backed away, that was enough for the match to end, sometimes in just a few seconds, without injury to either insect. But it wasn't always so gentle.

After each fight the little glass box was swept clean of any body parts left behind by the previous combatants and a new pairing was introduced. In due course I was invited to enter James Bond. He had been charging around in his cage for some time, seemingly agitated by all the commotion. He was ready for the fray, ready to kick some cricket butt, but when the time came to put him in the glass container to eye up his first opponent, my heart sank. He was half the size of the brute opposite him. Surely, I tried to suggest, there should be some weighing system — a welterweight cricket shouldn't have to front up in the super heavyweight division? But my complaints fell on deaf ears. James was dropped in and the partition went up. Someone went 'Eurghh!' when the big cricket pounced and bit off one of James's antennae like it was an entrée. I resisted the urge to reach in and rescue the poor little guy, knowing that this would probably bring shame upon him, but in the end I didn't have to worry: James had the situation fully under control. He had hopped back and was rattling his wings ferociously, emitting a loud, raucous chirruping that made the brute drop his half-eaten antenna and begin to have second thoughts of an easy contest. Now my worthy little cricket was pulling the only strategies he had going for him: cunning and guile. He stuck out a leg and limped forward a few centimetres, lowering his little head dismissively as his opponent advanced. Then, in a flash, he jumped and hit the big fellow broadside, chomping off a leg in the process. Before his opponent could react, James was neatly taking off the other main leg, leaving his rival with only its two pairs of front legs on which to make its escape. That was never going to be enough. It was all over as quickly as it had begun. James dealt the mortal blow a few minutes later, when he severed the head of the beast.

Or that's at least how I described the fight to Liu later that night when we were having dinner together. I thought the memory of my little cricket as a great champion should live on in at least someone's imagination, for only a bunch of Hui tribesmen and I knew the truth. Faced with a terrifying opponent nearly twice his size, James Bond had done what any smart cricket would do in the same circumstances: he'd done a runner. While the goliath had been busy nibbling on his right antenna, my brave little guy had emitted one last *chirrup*, hopped out of the box, zigzagged between the feet of the watching men and disappeared into a crack in the floor. Admittedly, I lost a reasonable chunk of money, but that in the end was more than compensated for by the happiness I felt for my cricket. He had won his freedom.

* * *

Our meal that night was eaten under the spluttering glow of a hurricane lamp that hung from a rafter over our heads. All of Xining was in darkness because of a power cut, the only light cast by lamps such as ours and the occasional diesel generator-powered bulb. Pools of luminescence were dotted along the streets and the town's inhabitants huddled within them: eating, drinking or playing card games to wile away the evening. Liu was in a thoughtful mood and wanted to talk about his country.

'How much do you know about China?' he began, lifting a bowl of rice to his lips and shovelling several loads into his mouth with chopsticks.

'I know you have a population of young people aged between 14 and 29 that is greater than the entire population of the USA,' I blurted out. 'I also know that there are more Chinese people standing on street corners waiting to cross the road than there are in all of Australasia. I read that somewhere — in a *National Geographic*, I think, in a doctor's waiting room.'

He nodded and absent-mindedly played with a chunk of tofu on his plate, pushing it around with a chopstick. There was a pregnant pause. I noticed on the wall behind his head a photo of Tiananmen Square in Beijing, with the owner of the restaurant standing in the foreground, his arm pointing towards the portrait of Chairman Mao above the gate to the Imperial Palace. Unfortunately, the angle the photo was taken at made it look as if the man's finger was stuck up Mao's nose.

'You are right, we have big problems in China,' Liu said finally. 'For the youth there is little hope of a good job. Everyone works so hard to get into a university, but maybe they end up in a factory all the same. We are so many.'

Liu was grimacing down at the table as an elderly woman brought fresh tea in a chipped pot. I asked if he had a solution to the problem and he leant forward, bending his neck down to my level.

'We get rid of this party of old men in Beijing,' he whispered.

I imagined the youth of China, all 297 million of them, marching on the capital city to take over. If they ever got together and acted as one, the change would be immediate. No army could hold back such a force. It would be over in a week. The only problem was, could they tear themselves away from their computer screens long enough to be bothered?

Liu sighed and poured the tea, first into my glass then his, as is the custom. Then he sat back and laughed.

'But it won't happen,' he said with the air of a confirmed fatalist. 'There is more chance of me playing for the Los Angeles Lakers.'

Just then the power came on and we sat blinking in the harsh blaze of electric light. People in the street gasped with relief as the oppression of the darkness was all at once lifted. Xining was working again like a well-oiled machine. Suddenly, Liu's cellphone started ringing.

'Careful,' I warned.

'Why?'

'Could be the Lakers calling.'

SEVEN

KUMBUM MONASTERY, AN ANCIENT RELIGIOUS CENTRE ALSO KNOWN as Ta'er Si, was at the head of a valley dotted with tall trees and purple flowering grasses. A cool wind had sprung up from the south, bringing with it the fresh high-altitude air of Qinghai's vast and lonely hinterland. In the summer the valley would bake under a relentless sun, turning into a dust bowl from which there was little escape. But for now the weather was perfect: warm sun and a gentle breeze, the lifelong friends of the long-distance traveller.

The bus that had brought me out here had been full when it arrived at the pick-up point on the eastern side of Xining. The passengers were peasants mostly, looking for blessings that would ensure a good harvest, and monks on pilgrimage seeking higher spiritual awareness. I was searching for a bit of both, particularly in the blessing department, although at first it didn't look too promising. The only seat available was a wooden box in the aisle. I looked through the gaps to see what was inside and the beady eyes of some chickens gazed back at me. They clucked nervously together, possibly wondering, as I was, whether the box would stand me sitting on it for a few hours.

Fortunately, though it creaked loudly at times, it held for the duration of our journey.

On arrival I followed the monks through the ticket office and up some stone steps towards one of the larger buildings. Kumbum is one of the six great Geluk 'Yellow Hat sect' monasteries of the Tibetan plateau and in its pre–Cultural Revolution prime would have been home to 3,000 monks. Now there were no more than 500 in residence, though from the noise they were making you'd have thought their number was still as strong. I could hear chanting and the banging of deep bass drums; every so often this would be intermingled with the clashing of cymbals so that the overall effect was both chaotic and ordered at the same time. There was routine in the sound: ancient repetition that gave the music an altogether otherworldly feeling.

I've been lucky enough to hear traditional instruments being played in many countries, from the two-stringed *tar* in Afghanistan to the *ney* flute of Arabia, but the solemnity and peacefulness of this music was wonderful. I sat down to listen in the sun, by an old wooden doorway carved with intricate geometric designs. It might have been the altitude or lack of sleep from the night before, or a mixture of both, but my eyelids soon grew heavy and I was powerless to stop them from closing …

* * *

In the dream I am walking again. It is always the same path each time, in every dream like this that I can recall, always through a field of harvested wheat in a dusty brown landscape of parched, rolling hills. I feel the crunch of stalks under my boots and find it pleasing, reassuring perhaps, because it is now so familiar. I have no idea where I am going, but I know for certain this is the way. One thing I also know is that I am rarely alone in this place. I am always here to meet someone, so it is not unexpected when the figure of an old man appears out of the heat haze on the path up ahead. I quickly make my way to where he is seated on a rock, waiting. He doesn't speak, but I can hear his words nonetheless as he looks to the sky.

'You see them?'

Way overhead, a flock of birds is flying in a perfect V-formation, heading south for the winter — the same direction as me. Their flight is effortless, in slow motion, as if gravity had no part to play in the equation. I know what it is instinctively: the allegory that reminds us we are better as a group than as a single unit. Flying in formation, each bird flaps its wings and creates uplift for the one immediately behind it, and so the whole flock increases its flying range by far more than if each bird flew alone.

'Is this message for me?' I think.

'No, not you,' comes the voice. 'Another.'

One of the birds breaks away and begins to head further west, but his flight appears slow in comparison to the rest. It's a struggle, as if the lone bird is now subject to unfavourable headwinds that don't affect the others. Yet still it carries on regardless.

'That is you,' comes the voice again, but this time it is full of sorrow and I am hearing once more the voice of my dead father. I turn to go and find the wheat stalks have suddenly grown into thick brush, thorny and impenetrable, and the path has vanished.

I yell out loud, 'What is happening?'

The old man stands up and gestures south, as a whirlwind dances at his bare feet, his long arm bent in the direction of the flock.

'Tell him,' he commands.

I yell against the wind. 'Tell him what?'

The response is immediate, but this time the voice is female, soft and unfathomably kind. There are only two words that I hear and they come to me just as I am waking.

'To forgive.'

* * *

There was no one around to talk to when I opened my eyes, no one to offer an explanation as to the meaning of the dream. I wondered whether it might have something to do with Liu for a moment, but the idea seemed unlikely. There was no connection between us other than the fact we had happened across each other's paths.

I rose to my feet and was surprised at how good I felt. Not tired, but more alive than before. My possessions were few, but I carried the burden of the task I had set myself, and now it seemed lighter. Self-doubt is a terrible travelling companion and, sometimes, though I had kept it to myself, I had despaired at the seeming impossibility of this journey and what I aimed to achieve. A voyage from A to B, the subject of nearly all successful travel books, including some of mine, is simple by comparison. Even if the distance between the two points is vast and the journey is beset with hardship and difficulty, it is still just an endurance test: put one foot in front of the other and the end will be reached. But what I was doing was partly investigative and required a new set of skills, one of which was patience — not my forte. Nevertheless, now, for the first time in a long while, I felt more at ease with what I was doing.

The smile on my face must have been obvious as I stepped over the wooden threshold and into a sort of anteroom with a ceiling that was open to the sky. To the left was a high wall of mud brick that had been plastered and whitewashed so that it shone brightly. To the right, a brick archway led into a courtyard of paved stone with a wooden staircase at one end that provided access to a second floor. The place seemed empty until there came the loud slapping of sandals on stone and a young monk appeared, running at full speed, red robes flying. He slowed down when he saw me, as if I might have chastised him for breaking some monastic rule about running in the corridors, so I asked him where he was going. He replied that it was time to eat, and dashed past me, out the way I had come in. I felt like an intruder at this point, a visitor who had outstayed his welcome. This part of the monastery was clearly the monks' living quarters and, as such, a private domain. I started to go, but then I saw a figure waving at me to come over.

He was an elderly monk, wrapped in a cloak of gold that showed a glimpse of the crimson cloth he wore underneath. In his hand was a simple bowl of rice and bread, which had no doubt been brought to him by the boy I had just met. He was sitting on a low, wooden bench on a landing halfway up the stairs and he patted the space beside him with fingers bent by age and arthritis.

'Tashi delek,' I said, using the common Tibetan greeting that means 'May all good and auspicious signs come to this location.'

His reply, however, was in polished German.

'Sprechen Sie Deutsch?' he said, asking if I could speak the language.

I laughed at the irony of it all. My German was better than my Tibetan or Mandarin, and so it was that I could communicate with a monk, in a Tibetan monastery, in China, in a completely different language from the ones we were both used to.

His name was Gonbo. When I asked him how old he was, he simply smiled and told me it didn't matter how many years he had lived, but how many times.

'And how many is that?' I asked.

'Not enough,' was his reply. 'Otherwise I would not still be here on this earth.'

He chortled at this and gathered the robes around his body to ward off the cold. There was not much of him to cover, though, and his bare arms were thin and wrapped in skin that seemed a size too big for his frame. It hung loosely from his face as well, and his eyes were deep in their sockets. Yet, despite these obvious signs of old age, his mind was razor sharp.

'Do you know Koblenz?' he asked.

'On the Rhine, yes,' I replied. 'I've been there a few times.'

He smacked his lips together in delight: 'Is that so? Then you'll know the castle on the hill overlooking the river — Ehrenbreitstein. I stayed there in 1960 for two years.'

The castle was one that I had stayed in too. It was a hostel in my time, though, run by an Austrian man who loved archery, Roman history and beer, in that order. He practised his archery by aiming his arrows skywards over the Rhine, pulling the drawstring tight across his ample belly in an attempt to hit the other side, where Roman enemies had once gathered. Sometimes a passing tourist barge would make a better target, however, and one day, after several litres of Pilsner, he'd struck a pilothouse, only narrowly missing the captain.

Gonbo explained how, after the Chinese invaded and occupied Tibet in the early 1950s and the Dalai Lama fled into exile in 1959, life for a monk was incredibly hard. He could not freely practise his religion without risking a beating from Mao's Red Guards, who favoured torture over imprisonment, and so he had followed his leader into exile, first trekking to Nepal then India, followed by Persia and Turkey before finally hiding himself aboard a train to Germany. There, he became a refugee and in time, courtesy of a wealthy German couple who lived near Koblenz in a tiny Westerwald village, found himself a new home.

But, he asked suddenly, what about me? Where did I come from? So I drew out my notebook and handed it to him, opening it to the first page, where Liu had written the explanation of my purpose in China. He fussed over it for some time, reading and re-reading certain lines before closing the book and handing it back.

'Now I understand,' he said. 'When I saw you sleeping there on the steps of our temple, I wondered about you. So you are not a Buddhist in search of enlightenment?'

I shook my head, feeling slightly guilty as I did so.

'That is good for you,' he carried on, unperturbed. 'Where you are going, they do not like Buddhists. In Qinghai and Sichuan province there will be no problem, people will be kind to you, but the further east you go, the further from safety you will travel. If you go to Hunan and Jiangxi, which of course you must,' he said, tapping the notebook, 'this is where you will find the red heart of China, and there they have no religion but Mao.'

Slowly the old monk got to his feet and stretched, then pulled a wooden staff from under his robes and began to descend the steps, one at a time. I followed dutifully, taking care not to tread on the crimson trailing edge of his clothing. When he reached the bottom, he turned around to face me.

'When do you go?' he asked.

I told him tomorrow.

'You know, you must ready your mind for this journey,' he said, running a crooked hand over the stubble of his shaven head. 'The roads are long and hard. In places the mountain passes might be closed, sometimes for days. The snows will come early this year too. I have seen the geese flying in great numbers already. They know. They always know.'

He then produced a small leather pouch, and from it retrieved a colourful slip of paper printed with Tibetan script.

'Om mani padme hum,' he said, putting the paper into my hand. 'The first three syllables stand for generosity (Om), belief (ma) and patience (ni). You will need them.'

'What about the meaning of the other three syllables?' I asked, slipping the folded paper into my shirt pocket.

Gonbo sighed. 'Patience,' he said, turning to go. 'The baby crawls before it walks.'

I sat on the bottom step and watched as he shuffled across the courtyard and out through the gate. The *click-clack* of his walking stick on the stone steps echoed loudly, before fading away.

EIGHT

During a previous journey in China, I had once survived three days and two nights in hard-seat class sharing a cramped wooden train seat with two other passengers, one a flea-ridden peasant and the other an off-duty policeman. (Hard-seat class was different from hard-sleeper. In the latter you had the luxury of a bunk, whereas in the former you slept sitting up, leaning against your immediate neighbour for support.) On the first night my old desert-coloured Iranian army bag, which I had carelessly left on the floor, had started to slide, seemingly of its own accord, under our seat. Seeing this, the policeman dived down after it with much shouting, emerging minutes later, covered in dust, clutching an even dustier thief. Not waiting for the train to stop, he simply thrust open the door and threw the culprit out into the darkness. The peasant's pleas for mercy were lost to the night.

From that day on, I've been aware that a Western traveller can cause problems simply by being in a world that is not their own. The thief, if that was indeed his profession, might not have been so sorely tempted had I been less imprudent. But therein lies the rub, of course: we dive into foreign cultures in search of new experiences but, in so doing, may create waves that have unintended consequences. Far better, therefore, to try and slip into those waters unnoticed, in disguise even. But that is sometimes easier said than done, especially when you walk with giants.

At the bus station the next morning, the first stage of the 800-kilometre journey to Yushu began. My intended route wasn't along the exact path of the Long March just yet, but instead ran parallel to it. For now, I was more interested in spending time with the Tibetans in this area of Qinghai province, in order to learn more about what they thought of Mao and how they viewed their role in his historic walk. As a people and a culture, they had not benefited greatly from the advent of Communism in China — far from it in fact. But, back in the time of the march, had they been friend or foe to the desperate rabble of Mao's followers as they sought to escape Chiang Kai-shek?

Liu had come to see me off and as usual he attracted a crowd of people. Those who were practising their tai chi, the elderly stretching their limbs and the young playing badminton: all came to gawp at the colossus. The other passengers on the bus climbed out of their seats to get a better look, some even went to touch Liu's clothing, just to make sure he was real. When we shook hands to say goodbye, my hand disappeared into his like a baby's hand enfolded by an adult's. He gave me his cellphone number and I wished him luck with the business. 'No problem,' he said. It would be 'fine and dandy'.

'Bob's your uncle,' I replied and, with that, I left him to his congregation of admirers.

* * *

The bus travelled west for the first part of the day, along a road lined with tall poplar trees and the occasional willow with its leaves starting to turn from green to gold. They were planting more trees in Qinghai. Even the multinationals were getting in on the act as a way of currying favour with the provincial government. Unilever, one of the largest of them all, had stuck thousands of dragon spruce and birch trees in the soil up near Qinghai Lake, to try and hold back the encroaching desert. Millions of dollars were being spent on this important project and expert analysis of local conditions meant the chosen species of trees were well suited to the high altitude. But no one told the local villagers, who promptly chopped them down for firewood.

Along the way we picked up more and more passengers, whose belongings were added to the growing pile in the space between the seats: bundles of blankets tied up with twine destined for a nomad's tent before winter set in; a new chainsaw, still in its packaging; and boxes containing live animals, in which the creatures defecated out of fear, so that the bus windows had to be opened to get rid of the stench. Sometimes, only the cargo came aboard and our journey was delayed as the Hui owners haggled tenaciously with the Han Chinese driver over the price of delivery.

'How much do you want? That is crazy! It is just to the next village! Half that amount would still be a crime.'

And so it went on. The driver always had the upper hand, as there were no other methods of delivery — he was it.

The driver had a young girl as his helper. She collected money and allocated the passengers their seats, even if that 'seat' was nothing more than a plastic stool in the aisle. She was slim and pretty, dressed in a pink top and denim shorts with a sunflower motif on the pockets, but when it came to dealing with anyone who stepped out of line she was as tough as they come. Those who tried to short-change her invariably ended up on the receiving end of an almighty tongue-lashing and, sometimes, a clip across the head for good measure.

Her name was Ping, or at least that was what she answered to whenever the driver needed something, or someone, sorted out. If the radiator needed topping up with water, it was Ping who fetched the container strapped to the top of the bus. If the driver felt hungry, it was Ping who peeled the fruit and fed it into his mouth. She was all things to all people, but one thing she wasn't was a pushover.

By the end of the morning we had turned south and were quickly gaining altitude. Xining and the populated world were left far behind as we journeyed over the vast grasslands, dotted here and there with the black tents of Amdo tribesmen. It was a glorious day. Blue skies stretched to all points of the compass and the sun streamed in through dusty windows.

At the back of the bus a game of cards was in progress, played by three villagers with tatty clothes and tobacco-stained teeth. At one stage a disagreement over a bet quickly turned sour, to the point where knives were drawn. But the matter was settled when the rest of the bus united together in a chorus of disapproval. It was just too nice a day for murder.

Not so glorious was the hideous creature who occupied the seat beside me. Her husband sat across the aisle eyeing me intently, suspicious that I might make a move on his woman. She was beyond ugly though, a veritable disaster area of knotted black hair and sulphurous breath, wearing layers of dirty green-and-orange robes tied together with a rope at her ample waist. The Tibetans are a noble race, with a handsome gene running through their line in most cases, but for her that line must have done a U-turn and gone someplace else. The odd thing was, her wary hubby across the way clearly couldn't see it. It occurred to me she might be rich, but judging by the state of her clothing it seemed unlikely. Maybe she had other talents that had captured his heart, but for the time being I just couldn't see any. It wasn't until later in the afternoon that her special gift was revealed.

A problem with the spare tyre meant we were all left sitting for several hours on the side of a dead straight road that was raised higher than the surrounding plateau by a couple of metres. Suddenly a beautiful voice began singing a wonderful folk song, and we all looked to see who it belonged to. It was my ugly neighbour from the bus who had walked down onto the grass below us, so that it appeared as if she stood on a vast stage that stretched to the horizon, while we were gathered in the circle. I discovered the songs were about a lover pining for her champion horseman, who was trapped in a far-off valley by a sudden snowstorm. Their separation would have to last through the winter, a long time in this part of the world, until spring could once again unite them.

The husband sat down next to me as if to say, 'See: am I not the luckiest guy in the world?' Just in case, he then gave me another one of his withering 'don't you even think about it' stares. I decided the best course of action was to give up my seat to him when we eventually climbed back on board, and this he graciously accepted. We became good friends after that, even to the point of sharing our food and water, and it was he who made the first entry in my notebook. At first he was reluctant to write anything, but I was insistent. It didn't matter that he had no knowledge whatsoever of Little Mao and precious little to say about any other subject relating to Mao himself, although this was to be expected given that so many others were listening in — in China candour could be foolhardy in the company of strangers. Nevertheless the notebook was soon being passed around the bus for everyone to read, just as I had hoped. Finally, after some time and much amusement, it came back to the front of the bus and was given to Ping.

'Read it,' said the driver abruptly, pulling another cigarette out of a pack with his lips. He was a large man but not tall — thick set in the way of wrestlers. He had been watching in his rear-view mirror and listening intently to the conversation.

Ping turned to the first page. The driver's eyes constantly flicked between the road and his attractive helper as she read aloud from the notebook. When Ping finished, he took it from her and checked it for himself. We drifted across the road towards a ditch and he was forced to swerve suddenly to avoid ending up in it.

For a moment I thought he might know something of use, but in the end his interest proved to be mere curiosity. Ping gave the book back to me and smiled sweetly.

'Do you speak Chinese?' she asked in Mandarin.

'A little,' I replied. 'Do you speak English?'

She shrieked with laughter and put a hand over her mouth, then retreated to her seat at the front. My guess was she spoke little English, although at her age she would probably already have sat through at least four or five years of English classes. This was one big change I'd noticed since my earlier visits to China: just how many of the younger generation could now communicate in basic English, providing they were brave enough to do so.

The breakdown had taken quite some time to fix and the afternoon was well on the wane by the time we reached the little village of Huashixia. The regulation pit stop was a welcome relief because we had been on the move for 12 hours. My water was all gone and the altitude was beginning to give me a headache. I sat on a low wall beside the bus and rested my head in my hands.

Huashixia was the home of my new acquaintances: the man and his sweet-sounding but not-so-sweet-looking woman. He walked up to me with a sack on his back, pointed at his head and let out a mock groan, as if his head was exploding. I nodded back and rubbed my temple. His medical diagnosis was right on the button. Above 2,500 metres, altitude sickness is one of the many things that can kill you (the others being more dramatic, like snow leopards and avalanches). It's 10 times worse than a hangover, and a very bad one at that, and is basically caused by insufficient oxygen reaching the brain. Symptoms include poor vision, doziness, vomiting, an inability to sleep and a head that feels like its gone one-on-one for 10 rounds with Muhammad Ali. There's no telling who will get it and there's no known cure.

The only wise thing you can do is ascend slowly to allow your body to adjust, and, if it strikes, retreat to a lower elevation as soon as possible. In my case I wasn't suffering any of the other symptoms, so I was happy to stay put and see it out.

'Come,' said the man, slipping his free hand under my arm to lift me up. 'Tea.'

Our burly bus driver was hunched over a plate of noodles outside a small roadside kitchen and didn't look like he was going anywhere for a while, so I followed the couple a short distance to a narrow street that climbed a hill beneath jagged cliffs of white stone.

The sun was low in the sky, its last rays making the sacred peaks of Amnye Machen glow a brilliant celestial white in the east. At one time this holy mountain was thought to be even higher than Everest. This was shortly after it had been brought to the attention of the Western world in 1921 by Brigadier-General George Edward Pereira, an experienced soldier and explorer known to his regiment as 'Hoppy', after he injured his leg in a riding accident. But a few decades later an American climbing team recorded the exact height as 6,282 metres, well short of the Everest mark. This, however, mattered not to the 10,000 Tibetans who continued to make the 200-kilometre pilgrimage around the base of the mountain each year. To the local Golok people and Tibetans worldwide, Machen was an earth god who controlled the rain, hail, thunder and lightning and was the protector of the Goloks, whose paradise floated above the mountain's blessed peaks. Machen would appear to them, sometimes in the guise of a handsome Tibetan shepherd, at other times as a fearsome deity. The Goloks were pretty fierce themselves and never shied away from cutting the throats of anyone who came close to their mountain, which may explain why it took so long to be discovered by the outside world. In the Tibetan language, Golok actually means 'head backward' or 'rebel', so they must not have cared two hoots about what Lhasa, Beijing — or anywhere else for that matter — thought of them.

The couple's home was a humble affair of sun-dried brick with a flat-topped roof supported by rough-hewn timber rafters gaily painted in blues and reds. We sat outside on wooden stools, the sun on our faces, as the wife brewed up what her husband indicated would be the perfect remedy for my complaint. She sang as she did so, a happy song that spoke of her delight to be home, and, after a few verses, appeared holding a glass that contained a brown, pungent liquid. It took some getting used to, but it was hot and thirst-quenching, so I didn't care. Two glasses later, I was feeling better. Three glasses later and the pounding in my head had diminished to a bearable throb. In the space of ten minutes, whatever it was they'd given me had brought about a rapid change. The old man showed me some dried roots that were tied in bunches to the wall of his house, as well as something that looked and smelt like a block of compressed animal dung. Mixed with hot water, this apparently had a magical, curative property and yet no special name was given to it. He simply said it was *ja*, or, in other words, 'tea'.

I poked my head inside to thank his wife and found her in the middle of the room beside a traditional stove with a flue that went straight up then angled to the side so that it exited the far wall beside a large portrait of a Buddhist deity. Around the stove were low bench seats, which made sense — the warmest part of the room is of course where you'd want to spend time eating — and there were other seats against the walls that were covered in colourfully decorated cushions, so the whole effect was quite cosy and comfortable. The floor was made of a dark timber and, in the far corner, a blanket hung down, possibly screening off the bedroom. The old man appeared behind me, pointed to it and chuckled to himself as if he were saying to me, 'And that my friend, is where the action happens.'

His wife giggled like a schoolgirl and went back to stirring the pot of *ja*. I might have stayed for another glass of the incredible stuff, if the blaring horn of the bus hadn't then sounded.

The journey continued through early evening and into a night illuminated by a full moon. When we finally reached Maduo we were too tired to speak, and instead the passengers collected their things in silence and drifted off into the darkness. The main street had a row of shops on each side, but the few streetlights showed them all to be shut and there was no sign of anywhere to stay. A group of dogs outside a mechanic's shop watched me walk a short distance, then scattered when a shout came from behind. It was Ping, waving from the doorway of an innocuous-looking two-storey building. It didn't look much like a hotel but in my weary state I didn't care. It had a room on the second floor with a single bed and a massive duvet folded at one end, as well as a few extra blankets printed with colourful geometric patterns of red and gold. It wasn't quite cold enough for the duvet, so I simply left my clothes on and crawled under the blankets, knowing that another long day of travel lay ahead. Maduo was only halfway to Yushu, and Yushu was the place where I would eventually leave Qinghai province and finally pick up the trail of the Long March, before following it back to the point where it all started. Yushu was, I felt, a sort of crossroads, when things would start to get progressively more serious in terms of the success or failure of my journey.

Sleep took over in minutes and, when I opened my eyes again, it was morning.

* * *

I splashed water onto my face from a cracked porcelain sink in the bathroom down the hall, while another guest washed his underwear in the one opposite. The toilets were open cubicles perched over a single drain, down which water from a tap at the far end sluiced the contents. On the way back I stopped to look out a row of windows that faced the rising sun. The warmth felt good, though I could tell from the vaporous breath emanating from a lone yak in the street below that the temperature outside had dropped in the night. He or she — one can never tell with a yak — was munching on the aerial of a 4WD parked at the back of the hotel. It was then I noticed the door to one of the rooms was ajar behind me. Inside, a young Chinese man in his late twenties was rubbing his eyes while sitting on the edge of his bed. He stretched.

'Is that your car?' I asked.

Maybe my Mandarin wasn't quite clear, because he looked at me quizzically. So I clutched an invisible steering wheel, made a roaring sound and then pointed outside. This time he smiled and nodded, and said something to another person in the room, who laughed. The car was a nice one, a Jeep Cherokee, and so I guessed he took me for an admiring observer. Seconds later, another Chinese man appeared, ten years older than the first, holding a towel in one hand and a shaving brush in the other. Seeing me in the hall, he hitched up his pyjama bottoms.

'Your car,' I said again. 'Bu yao! Not good!'

He stepped sleepily forward into the hall and peered outside to where I was pointing. Seeing the yak contentedly eating his aerial, he immediately sprang to life and raced down the stairs, still clutching the drawstring of his pyjamas and shouting out what I could only imagine was a Mandarin version of 'Shoo!' The sight of him waving the yak away had his friends, including, now, a young woman from the room next door, in hysterics. They doubled up with laughter as they watched the battle down below, which ended only when the yak decided metal wasn't all that tasty after all and ambled off to greener pastures. The upshot of all this, however, was that I had made a friend for life — or friends for that matter — and soon my attentiveness was richly rewarded with the offer of a ride further west, in the very same vehicle I had helped save.

They were a group of travellers from Xi'an: two men in their mid-twenties from Xi'an University; Wei, the 30-something owner of the vehicle, who wore white driving gloves, made all the decisions concerning their route and carried a Hasselblad camera; and the young woman, who turned out to be the bright spark in the group. She introduced herself and asked me to join them for breakfast while Wei fixed his aerial.

We packed and went downstairs to a teahouse where there was a wooden table by the window in the sun. The owner appeared from behind lace curtains and we ordered bowls of hot rice soup and a few hard-boiled eggs. He said it would take a while because he wasn't open yet and the fire was still unlit, then he shuffled back the way he had come. I heard a back door slam shut and a waft of cold air made the curtains screening his kitchen dance. As we waited, the girl explained that they were on their first trip outside of Xi'an and had hired Wei and his 4WD for the fortnight. Her name was Hua, which meant 'flower', she said, before tilting her head back and laughing loudly. I soon discovered Hua did this a lot. She lived to make fun of the others and to tease them about what they were wearing or something they had said. Everything was a joke to her, and for that reason I liked her. So many Chinese expressed a serious, slightly downtrodden view of life, whereas Hua sought out the frivolous and fatuous in everything. I wondered whether her parents were of the well-heeled entrepreneurial variety, making Hua a child of China's new business elite. Xi'an was a prosperous tourist city after all, home to the second century BC Terracotta Warriors. My suspicions were later confirmed when I discovered that the Hasselblad camera, one of the most expensive you can buy, was hers and not Wei's. He was simply its self-appointed 'minder'.

The watery soup arrived with a pair of hard-boiled eggs that were small and spotted. We slurped communally until Wei pulled up outside, gunning the engine impatiently. This was the signal to drain our bowls and pay the bill, a share of which I was not allowed to contribute, no matter how much I protested. Then I was shown into the front passenger seat of the Jeep no less, while Hua and the two men squeezed into the back. Compared to the beaten-up old bus I'd spent the previous day in, this was extreme luxury. There was even a digital altimeter stuck to the dashboard that also registered the angle of our vehicle. It showed we were on a perfectly flat surface, 4,267 metres above sea level. Wei gunned the engine once more, selected first gear with his right, gloved hand, and we were on our way.

Except that the journey was over almost immediately. We had gone only a couple of metres when the front of the Jeep suddenly plummeted into a hole in the street. I looked at the altimeter, which indicated we were now at an angle of 45 degrees. How Wei, or any of us, for that matter, could have missed the hole was hard to fathom. It was the size of a spa pool. And we were stuck fast in it.

No one was hurt though, and the only damage was to Wei's not-insignificant ego. A group of Tibetans made sure the entire village turned out to see the stupid Han and his truck, with its rear wheels spinning helplessly in the air. They pointed and laughed, and brought chairs out from the teahouse so that they could sit and watch. This was clearly better than a Jackie Chan movie on a Friday night. One man brought a donkey and the hapless animal was made to strain impossibly at the task of freeing the vehicle. Half an hour later an empty lorry rolled through town and the young driver was persuaded to help. He was Tibetan too, with cheeks rubbed raw by the elements, and he had just come from delivering a supply of frozen yak meat to a nearby monastery. 'Nearby', I learnt, was 200 kilometres away.

Fortunately, with the lorry pulling and a couple of us pushing, the 4WD gained the traction it needed to reverse back out, but not without a disturbing crunching noise coming from its undercarriage. Once the car was back on the road, we saw that the right front wheel was turned in at an unnatural angle and the tyre had burst. A wizened elder tapped the wheel, then spat into the dust, indicating to the assembled onlookers that it was fixable, but the prognosis for a quick repair was not good.

Back in the teahouse, I surveyed my options while Wei sulked in the corner, smoking cigarette after cigarette and leaving the butts on the floor. Hua was upbeat, however.

'You know, the truck driver has asked me if I would like a lift with him to the next village. He can take one other. You?'

'What about Wei and your two friends,' I replied, sensing something more in her invitation than just a simple ride. 'Won't they be sad?'

'They are boring! But I like the foreigner man.'

She smiled and showed off a row of perfect teeth, before pouring out a cup of green tea for each of us. There were things I noticed about her then that I hadn't paid much attention to before. She was young, yes, but in the excitement of finding a ride I hadn't really taken in just how attractive she was. Straight black hair framed a petite, heart-shaped face. Her eyes were bright and seemed to shine even more when she laughed. No wonder, I thought, that the truck driver had offered her a lift. She was gorgeous, and what's more she knew it. And somehow Hua made it seem quite okay to use her looks in this way. It was as if they were a currency she was well used to dealing in, and no doubt they bought her entry to places she would not normally have reached. Men, I could see her thinking, were such easy prey.

I toyed with the idea of declining her offer and then thought better of it. A ride was a ride after all, and I was eager to get going. So I agreed, and left Hua to tell the others what was happening. Whether they would like or dislike the plan I had no idea, but within minutes Hua and I were climbing into the front seat of the lorry, bound once more for the high-altitude vastness of the Qinghai countryside.

The next part of the journey was especially beautiful. Deep valleys followed sparkling turquoise rivers rich in glacial sediment, here and there lined with trees that were hurriedly turning to gold before winter set in. Then we would rise up onto a flat plain, on a dead-straight road under a sky of cobalt blue.

At one stage our journey was interrupted when we pulled over to let the driver, Jamtso, relieve himself on the side of the road, during which he suddenly became very excited and started barking like a dog at something 50 or 60 metres away. With his free hand he frantically waved us over and we duly joined him, a discreet distance from where he was watering the earth, to see what he could see. At first I couldn't spot a thing because what he was looking at was so cleverly camouflaged, but then the ground moved and the grey-brown outline of a Tibetan fox came clearly into view. It must have thought us a comical sight: the Westerner, the pretty Chinese girl and the peeing Tibetan driver, all three intently watching his every move. Then, as if bored, it turned and made off across the grassland, perhaps looking for a tasty marmot. Jamtso cleared his throat loudly, zipped himself up and spat out a glob of mucus. On his way back to the truck he smiled at Hua and started singing a Tibetan love song in a shrill voice. He was happy, no doubt proud of his ability to spot a rare beast in the wild, and content also that he was master of his ship, with its crew of two upon the highest ocean of the world.

Only the happiness was abruptly replaced with a scowl when the ship would not start again. While he fussed with the engine, I chatted with Hua.

'You're very brave,' I said.

'Why?' she replied, with an almost hurt expression.

'To leave your friends and travel with strangers, of course. Your mother would be worried if she knew, I bet.'

'Are you a bad person?'

'No.'

'Are you going to steal my money?'

'Of course not,' I said, suddenly being the one to feel hurt.

'Are you going to try and kiss me against my will?'

I said nothing and laughed, realising I was being played by a first-rate, serial tease. Hua enjoyed this and laughed too, coquettishly, but in a way that seemed very slightly tinged with annoyance. With arms folded, she looked out the window: 'Then what is there for my mother to be worried about?'

Fortunately there was a loud thump on the bonnet just then and Jamtso appeared below, asking me to turn the ignition. I was only too happy to jump into the driver's seat and thus extricate myself from an increasingly tetchy Hua. I pumped the accelerator, depressed the clutch and turned the key to a chorus of mechanical approval as the engine roared into life. If only people could be as simple, I thought, and slid back into the middle seat.

We drove on in silence for the rest of the morning. Jamtso appeared to be nursing an ailing motor, because he rolled in neutral down even the slightest slope. At times I could have got out and walked at a faster rate, but then he would gently select a gear and our speed would climb again. All the while, the view outside the window never changed from the vast grassland that makes up so much of the Qinghai plateau. Some areas were waterlogged and tall-legged birds stepped cautiously through reeds, ever alert for their next meal. About midday, I noticed a group of black tents off to one side, the distinctive dwellings of nomadic Kham tribesmen. There was no one around, the only movement coming from the coloured flags attached to the tents, which fluttered urgently in the wind. Then, a few kilometres further on, a lone figure appeared, trotting on horseback towards us. We slowed down as he approached, and Jamtso put the engine into neutral so that we coasted to a halt.

The rider appeared to be about 50. A gap-toothed smile welcomed us from beneath a felt hat like a cowboy's, sides turned up and brim pulled down. However, there was something about him I didn't trust, something that under normal circumstances would have made me not only want to leave the room he was in, but also the general district. Jamtso wound his window down and leant half out of it, speaking rapidly in Tibetan. By interpreting the facial expressions and gesticulations of both men, I understood the conversation to be this:

'Hey friend, do you have a spare C-50 distributor cap for a 1975 Dongfeng on you?'

'A C-50? That could be tricky.'

'I'll trade you an hour with the Chinese girl, or you can shoot the Westerner I have in my truck and feed him to your pigs.'

'Now that you mention it, I do seem to recall seeing a C-50 in the tent. Why don't you follow me down this deserted dirt road and we'll do a deal.'

'Good. Lead the way.'

There are times when every bone in your body says 'run', but all you can do is sit there meekly. It's not a frozen-to-the-spot kind of fear, but a 'this is all happening too swiftly to make an adequate judgment' sort of feeling, topped off with a 'if I jump out now and I'm wrong, I'm going to look really stupid' sense of unease. This was just such a time.

The truck backed up a few metres, then turned right off the tarmac and headed down a dusty track towards a low hill that, as we drew nearer, was revealed to be the site of a motley collection of black felt tents. We pulled up to the central one and, much to my dismay, Jamtso was quick to get down and continue his conversation with the lone rider, this time out of earshot, and not without several telling gestures in our direction. I decided offence was going to be the best line of defence, so I got out of the truck with my camera and started to take pictures of the horseman, who puffed out his chest and struck a noble pose. As I clicked away, I noted somewhat comfortingly the absence of any pigsty. Soon, a tent was made available to us. The flap was thrown back and Hua and I were given a low stool each to perch on. Minutes later a stinking broth of curd was brought in by Jamtso. Hua took one sip and almost choked.

'Poison!' she grimaced.

Quietly, I hoped not. I looked around me. The tent was a single room, with bedding stacked neatly against one wall. A rug covered the floor and a pair of hurricane lamps hung from each of the two wooden supporting poles. The tent billowed in and out constantly, as if it were breathing. It was dark and dreary.

'Do you think this will take long?' Hua asked, sounding uncomfortable, and putting her bowl on the floor.

'I have no idea. I think — at least I hope — not long, maybe a few minutes.'

I stared at the sunlight coming through the opening in the tent, so that when the wind suddenly whipped the tent flap shut everything went very dark. Hua shrieked. I dropped the bowl and leapt to my feet, eyes adjusting too slowly to the blackness, fumbling forward to where I thought the door would be — and tripped over her, sending us both sprawling. We ended up in a heap on the rug, Hua on her back and me on top, trying not to squash her, while she tried to suppress a fit of the giggles. I was just starting to appreciate the humour of this Laurel and Hardy moment when the flap of the tent whipped back again, light poured onto our intimate embrace, and there was Jamtso, holding a bunch of electric wires and a screwdriver. He didn't say a thing, just backed out and retreated to his truck.

We emerged a few seconds later, still laughing, to find him behind the wheel and gunning the engine. There was no sign of the other Tibetan, but clearly any thoughts of a more sinister outcome to our visit were well and truly vanquished. We ran for the truck and jumped in as Jamtso ground the gears, selected first and sped off down the track. Before long the hum of tarmac was under our wheels again. Jamtso sang quietly to himself, but his tune had changed to a mournful song of loss and betrayal.

* * *

About the time England was winning the soccer World Cup for the first and only time, against West Germany in 1966, the Cultural Revolution was in full swing, its chief and unwavering purpose being the destruction of the 'four olds' — old habits, old customs, old culture and old thinking — and the birth of Mao's utopian future. No part of China was left untouched, but in Qinghai province perhaps the worst of all crimes were committed. Monasteries were torn down and monks were 'persuaded' to join the Red Army to help hunt down those Tibetans not aligned with the new way of thinking. Some of them cooperated, out of fear for their lives, but many refused to participate and suffered terribly as a result. Torture was commonplace. So-called *thamzing*, or 'struggle sessions', were a form of political re-education that involved public humiliation and, at worst, beheading, disembowelling or even being buried alive.

I asked Hua what she knew about this period and, not unsurprisingly, she regurgitated the official story that had been taught to her and millions of others, depicting a time of struggle that led to the formation of the great and glorious China of today. Tibetans were 'set free from serfdom and slavery under their feudal masters', and enjoyed numerous benefits under the Mao regime. I asked her what these were specifically, to which she replied:

'Freedom from serfdom and slavery under their feudal masters.'

I sighed. But, there I was, sandwiched between two people whose parents had lived through these years, albeit in very different circumstances given that Hua's family were most likely spared the kind of treatment meted out to the Tibetans. So I asked Jamtso the same question. His reply was fascinating, but provoked a curt response from Hua.

Jamtso: 'The Red Guards came and shot many people in my village.'

Hua: 'Clearly they were terrorists.'

Jamtso: 'My father's cousin was not a terrorist. He looked after the horses.'

Hua: 'Then he must have been attacking the guards, and so they were forced to defend themselves.'

Jamtso: 'He was not attacking anyone. He was asleep in his bed at the time, next to his wife and children. That's where they shot him.'

Hua: 'Why would the Red Guards do that? Kill a defenceless man? No, perhaps he had knives under his pillow, and lunged at the soldiers in order to slit their throats.'

Jamtso said nothing. The muscles in his jaw tightened as he clenched the wheel and looked straight ahead, his eyes tiny slits of rage. His self-control was remarkable, though Hua failed to take any of this in. She was lost in her own world of self-deception.

'Yes,' she said finally, 'that must be it. Lunged with daggers drawn in the darkness. It would have been very frightening.'

The peaceful Buddhist in Jamtso was fighting with his Tibetan side, which probably wanted to stop the truck and chuck her out, but I think even he realised the extent of her ignorance was a product of the school system and nothing more. He was older than her by ten years or so, in his early thirties, and had learnt forgiveness. Still, I couldn't help but look upon Hua as a silly little girl from then on, with brash ideas and a boldness that would one day get her into trouble. The Han Chinese apparently think of themselves as vastly superior to the other ethnic groups, and it was this bullshit manner that had wrecked so many lives, from here in Qinghai to the far western reaches of Xinjiang province. There, the local Uighur people had been forced to accept Han dominion over their government, businesses and schools. Their way of life was slowly eroding under the weight of Han migration, while the national government in Beijing promoted a tourist-friendly, multicultural face to the world, a sham of pretty ethnic costumes worn by 'approved' models. The Cultural Revolution was said to have lasted a decade, ending in 1976. But, truth be known, it was still alive and well in these remote western regions.

* * *

In the late afternoon we rumbled into Yushu, a small town of predominantly Tibetan people, which was situated at the juncture of two valleys, with a narrow river sweeping through the middle. At around 4,000 metres in elevation, it is one of the highest inhabited areas in the province. Jamtso dropped us off near a gargantuan monument to the famous Tibetan warrior, Gesar, built by the Chinese in an attempt to keep the locals happy. Red-robed monks walked beneath its mighty shadow on the way to their various monasteries.

Yushu was about as far west as you could go without running into an army patrol on the Tibetan border. Out there in that desolate landscape, if you survived the altitude, the treacherous roads and the cold, you still had to run the gauntlet of a security force hellbent on preventing anyone creeping into the Tibet Autonomous Region unannounced. Yushu was the back door to Tibet, the road few dared venture upon, especially now that there were more leisurely entry points into this once-closed kingdom, including a brand new, air-conditioned, atmospherically pressurised railway carriage that took people all the way from Chengdu to Lhasa, via Golmud in the north. That said, it wasn't a route I intended taking. Not on this trip anyway.

Yushu was for me, an important stage in the journey, as it marked the point at which I turned south to follow the route of the Long March in reverse. Though Tibet was an attractive target, even greater challenges lay ahead on the mountainous road into Sichuan province.

For the moment, though, I put my plans to one side while I worked out what to do with Hua. For my benefit, she pointed out a sign above a clothes shop that advertised single rooms at a bargain rate. Her guide, Wei, had already booked her and the rest of her party a room each in the far more regal hotel further down the street, which was much more suited to her budget and her liking. So I carried her bags to the entrance and arranged to meet her later the next day. I still had not talked to her about Mao and whether she knew anything of the boy; something told me it wouldn't be much.

My room belonged to the clothes-shop owner, who did a roaring trade selling crimson robes to the monks. He himself wore brown suit trousers and a white business shirt with no tie, while on his feet were a pair of open-toed sandals. He called himself Pai Mei, after a character in the Quentin Tarantino movie *Kill Bill: Vol. 2*, and spoke a halting English, picked up from the occasional tourist, he said. Tourists didn't come through Yushu much at this time of year. I asked how many he would see in the height of the season and he threw his arms out wide as if calculating a vast number, then said, 'Ten, maybe twelve.'

'Per day?' I asked.

'No, per year.'

The wooden steps at the back of the shop went up two flights to a narrow corridor with a bathroom at the end. There were three rooms, each with a single bed and a table, although in one there was also an ornately carved wooden bowl for washing in. He tapped it and pointed out the window at the monastery.

'The monks made it,' he said. 'Sometimes they have no money, so they pay in other ways. But I prefer money.'

I was the only guest, so I handed him several days' rent. He took the money, flicked through the notes with a practised ease, then folded them in half and slipped the wad deep into his trouser pocket.

'If you like,' he said. 'I can give you good price on some nice robes. Very nice material, excellent quality.'

'Where do they come from?'

'China,' he said, before adding slightly guiltily, 'But I don't tell that to the monks.'

Just then a bell rang in the shop below, summoning him downstairs in hot pursuit of another customer.

A Tibetan man on the road to Maduo

In Yushu, a look of sheer defiance

NINE

At dawn, the smell of cooking fires permeated the air and I went down to the street expecting to see someone roasting a yak. There was indeed a yak, but it was the living and breathing kind, feasting on some leftover vegetables in an alleyway. Lifting my gaze towards the 500-year-old Jiegu Monastery that overlooked Yushu, I soon spotted telltale smoke trails coming from its kitchens. The wind was blowing gently from that direction, bringing with it the delicious aroma of breakfast.

With nothing better to do, I started to walk towards the monastery via a series of narrow streets packed with houses on either side. Most had high walls and tall iron gates that accentuated the feeling of being hemmed in. A few lazy dogs watched me pass, but for the most part there was little sign of life. It was cool and the air was crisp, so I stuck my hands in the pockets of my jacket and trudged on. Soon the path up the mountain became clearly visible, breaking away from the houses and zigzagging its way up the steadily steepening slope.

After an hour or so, just as the sun appeared over the jagged horizon, I reached the rows of tall white stupas that lined the entrance to the monastery. Inside was an open area where a few dogs were hanging round a silver late-model Hyundai Tucson. One growled and took a few steps towards me, then it was joined by several more of its friends until they had fanned out across the courtyard, blocking my way. I don't like dogs, and unfortunately it seems that wherever I go in my travels there are always plenty of them. The ferocious mastiffs of Afghanistan struck greater fear into my heart than Russian gunships, although at least I knew those dogs had been trained since puppyhood to fear a well-thrown rock — nail the biggest one, preferably in the head, and the rest of the pack might leave you alone. But these guys I wasn't sure about, and the courtyard was swept clean of ammunition. I was considering turning back when a small boy in monk's robes suddenly appeared from one side and flew at the dogs, yelling and screaming and waving a large stick in front of their noses. They immediately scattered for the safety of unseen pathways.

When the boy saw me standing there in my blue jeans, thigh-length olive green coat and walking boots, he uttered a somewhat surprised greeting in Tibetan, then stuck a hand over his mouth and giggled at his mistake.

'Hello,' he finally said, having collected himself. 'I am pleasing to meet you.'

'I am pleasing to meet you too,' I replied. 'May I come in?'

Tsongpa, as I soon discovered, was about ten years old and it was his job that morning to clean the head lama's Hyundai. His intervention hadn't been a premeditated rescue, just a timely arrival. I was certainly grateful nonetheless.

I looked around and took in the buildings. On either side were some small houses separated by alleyways. At the far end, towering over the Hyundai, was a 20-metre-high red-washed wall; the top three metres or so were painted a darker brown and inset with large, circular shields of gold. Just visible over the wall was a golden roof, probably belonging to the main temple.

Tsongpa led me down one of the side paths to where a group of older monks were gathered on some stone steps that led into a large meditation hall. They appeared to be in their late twenties and were quite surprised to see the young boy return so soon. One of the monks frowned as if about to scold the boy, but relented when I came into view. They all got to their feet and shook my hand, then for a while we all stood around not quite knowing what to do next. In the end, Tsongpa was sent off to make some tea and we sat on the steps and communicated in silence. I speak hardly any Tibetan, and they knew only a few words of English, but somehow we managed to communicate. One monk in particular was quite loud and raucous. When I performed a mime to explain how I had come to China and then Qinghai province, he bellowed with laughter and shook my hand vigorously.

Tsongpa reappeared with a glass of hot tea, which tasted pretty good, and a piece of *tsampa* bread, made from roasted barley, which didn't. I thanked him anyway and he beamed with delight, before he was tersely reminded that the boss's car was still dirty. He scampered off in the direction of the courtyard to find a bucket and some water.

From within the meditation hall came the clink of chimes and the tapping of drums, prompting the monks to ready themselves for prayer. The loud one pulled out a cellphone from under his robes and switched it to silent mode, much to the others' amusement. Before going inside, however, he showed me a picture he'd taken with the phone's camera. It was of another temple, set into a dramatic cliff face and named after Wencheng, a seventh-century princess. He was most insistent that I should visit it with him, though exactly when was unclear. I simply nodded in agreement as he hurried up the steps with the other monks.

Departing soon after, I walked back down to the village accompanied by the sound of gongs and murmured incantations. I resolved to go to the Temple of Princess Wencheng the next day, with or without the monk. In the meantime, I would spend the rest of this day getting a feel for the area.

Under a brilliant blue sky, I wandered the streets and poked my nose into all sorts of nooks and crannies. Sometimes I received an immediate welcome from those I encountered; at other times I was met with a steely glare. The very young usually followed me about so closely that I resembled the Pied Piper. If I stopped suddenly, they crashed into the back of my legs.

At one restaurant where I sat down for dinner, I was watched attentively by a group of Tibetan lads in wide-brimmed felt hats and traditional Tibetan coats. They had movie-star looks, with high cheekbones and long black hair. In their belts they carried long knives in richly adorned scabbards. They were like armed peacocks.

I heard someone call my name and turned to find Hua at the doorway. She came in and sat opposite me. Out of the corner of my eye I saw the boys paying us even more attention.

'I'm tired,' she said.

'Of Yushu?'

'No, just tired from the trip. I've spoken to the others and they will be here tomorrow.'

'How do you know?' I asked, somewhat surprised, and she laughed at me mockingly.

'Cellphone, of course.'

I still couldn't quite get used to the fact that even in remote regions like this there was now cellphone coverage. This wasn't the China I remembered from my previous visits, a country isolated from modern inventions to such a degree that it still used steam-age machinery. The China of old had been cloaked in a soft mystique that had since, with the passing of time and the spread of technology, hardened into a much less romantic reality.

We talked about Hua's life in Shanghai as a child, before her father was given a teaching post in Xi'an. When her family arrived there, they discovered the school had been demolished to make way for a new hotel. Fortunately, Hua's father managed to find work at the hotel, once it was built, and after many years became its manager. Hua had no brothers or sisters: she was the sole recipient of all her parent's love and adoration, not to mention wealth.

'Do you work?' I asked.

'I am student. But I do not like to get a job. I want to marry a handsome man and have a family. My father has already picked someone out for me, but he is *boring*!'

Her eyes widened to add emphasis. She then cast a coy look over her shoulder at the group of wild, young Tibetans in the corner.

'Maybe one of these boys,' I suggested.

'No,' she said with a grimace. 'I do not like milking yaks.'

* * *

Later, in the thin night air, I lay on my bed trying to get back to sleep, listening to the sound of the cold river clattering by somewhere outside. It was 3 a.m. High altitude changes the air pressure in the lungs and always makes sleeping through the night more difficult, even if the body is exhausted. I'd often wake around this time and then have to wait for the dawn. At this hour, the mind plays tricks. The challenges I faced in finding the boy appeared bigger; the improbable started to seem impossible.

I switched on a torch and let the beam play across the walls, finding a stain in the corner from a leak in the roof, a mirror on a nail, and a picture of Yushu in the spring, with alpine flowers growing profusely. The image filled me with a new hope and I decided not to lie there dwelling on my seemingly slender chances of success. The solution, I knew, was to get up and start walking. So I slipped on my clothes, laced up my boots, wrapped myself in my warm coat and crept silently out the back door.

I'd discovered that the Temple of Princess Wencheng was a 40-minute taxi ride out of town or a 13-kilometre hike that followed the river. There was plenty of time to walk and so I decided to head in that direction.

The river was there before me, flowing steadily, unwavering in its goal. I began to pick my way along its edge. It was difficult at first because there were houses and fences in the way, but once I was free of Yushu I was able to more easily follow its winding path. Small animals scurried into their burrows as I approached; eyes reflected in the light from my torch. Were they the eyes of cats, I wondered, or foxes, or marmots, or deer perhaps, drinking from the same river I was navigating by? It was difficult to get an idea of their size or shape; only their presence could be sensed.

An hour passed, then two. The pre-dawn light filled the valley with a ghostly hue. I passed a small cottage built directly on the riverbank, but it was empty save for a family of mice and the smell of dung. Further on was an old swing bridge connecting a path that ran down from the hills to my left then continued on the other side of the river. I checked the ground around me for any sign of footprints that would suggest the bridge was still in use, but there were none to be seen. The wooden planks creaked when I put some weight on them, but held, so I took another step and then another. Quite soon I was at the halfway point and the bridge swung gently as I looked down into the water below. It was perhaps only a metre or two deep, no more I thought. If I fell, I'd only get wet. A little further on I came to the last section, where the planks weren't tied down but simply sat loosely upon the cables. There were ten or twelve boards like this, spanning the last three or four metres of the bridge, all the way to the opposite bank. When I'd crossed them and reached the safety of dry land again, it struck me as odd that no one had bothered to secure them firmly.

Soon the dawn light slid down the mountainsides and a blue sky replaced the early-morning grey. Because the path followed the river I stuck to it, wondering where it might lead. At times, where the river turned a corner sharply and a small but steep cliff was formed, the path diverted round and over the rocky headland, but for the most part the way was unerringly smooth.

I lost track of time and simply trudged on, enjoying the solitude immensely, feeling at peace. I wondered whether, long ago, this same path had seen the passing of Red Army feet, fleeing the Nationalist soldiers or marauding Tibetans who would not have welcomed these strangers to their lands. The lucky ones would have worn boots while the less fortunate hobbled along in sandals made of rough twine. Whenever the former fell, through sickness or deathly exhaustion, they were set upon by the others and their boots were ripped from their bodies with hardly a word said. A good pair of shoes was worth its weight in gold in Mao's military, even more so than a rifle. Not that the Communist forces were poorly equipped. On the contrary, they carried the latest weapons: German, British or American machine guns and ammunition, nearly always captured from enemy troops. What they also had on their side was youth. Their average age was 19, while their commanders were hardly much older, yet many had already experienced several years of fighting, after joining up in their early teens. Most came from the land: they were the sons of hardy farmers who could work all day on a handful of rice or a bowl of soup made from bark. They were slender of build, but stout of mind.

The members of the Red Army were fighting not only for their lives, but for their homes and their country. They never called themselves *ping*, or 'soldiers', but used the term *chan-shih*, which translates as 'fighters' or 'warriors'. This, together with their evident skill and bravery, created a mystique that played upon the minds of their enemy. Many Nationalist soldiers began to believe the Communists were invincible; often they would surrender without a fight or even, in some cases, change sides and join the Communist ranks. It was only the very best of Chiang Kai-shek's army that could be trusted to follow orders. And even then they would return and tell stories of their foes, how the Reds ran at their lines with such fierce determination, their regimental commanders standing shoulder to shoulder, in the heat of battle, with the lowest rank-and-file recruits.

* * *

The tiny Temple of Princess Wencheng, named after a Tang Dynasty Chinese princess who married King Gampo of Tibet and converted him to Buddhism, was tucked in against the side of a cliff just beyond a narrow gorge, which eventually opened out into a wide, bowl-shaped valley. Overhead, lines of colourful prayer flags bearing sutras, the holy scriptures believed to be the teachings of Buddha, stretched from one side of the gorge to the other and festooned the mountainsides. Higher up on the cliffs, small meditation retreats had been built into every available crevice, like eagles' nests; the steps that climbed to them precipitously were hewn from the very rock.

 The river I had been following had created the gorge over millions of years. No doubt it had provided water for the 16-year-old princess when she paused here in about 641 AD en route to her wedding to King Gampo in the Tibetan capital of Lhasa. It would also have served to cool the aching muscles of her entourage, who had already carried her for so long and still had so far to go. Clearly she was in no hurry, because the poor king had to wait three years for her to arrive; though once she did, Wencheng became a formidable force in Tibet, founding some of Lhasa's greatest monasteries and temples.

I crunched across the gravel path and came to wooden doors in the outer wall of the temple. They were locked. I banged on them, but no one came. It was then I noticed a pilgrimage path, or *kora*, leading up onto the mountain. Thinking that perhaps the temple would open later, I set out on the steep climb and it wasn't long before I was high enough to get a panoramic view. I found a rocky ledge, worn smooth as silk by the centuries of passing Tibetan feet on the clockwise circumambulation of this temple, stretched out in the sun and, finally, fell fast asleep.

It was the sound of voices that woke me some hours later. I sat up and saw three monks approaching the *kora*, quickly mounting its steps. There was a van parked outside the temple; soon after I heard the engine rev and it turned around to leave via a road through the gorge. When it had gone, silence filled the valley again, except for the chattering of the three men — or, should I say, the chattering of one monk, because the lead man was doing all the talking. As soon as I realised that, I recognised him: he was the same fellow I had met at the monastery above Yushu — the loud, talkative one with the cellphone.

'Tashi dele,' I said, once they were only a few metres below me.

'Tashi de—' They stopped almost in unison, then broke out in a chorus of welcome. There was much handshaking and backslapping, mostly from the loud one, whom I soon came to know was called Tenzin, after the fourteenth Dalai Lama. The other two were Dawa, who was a short, stout, bull of a man, and Sopa, who smiled a lot and wore a yellow hat. At their insistence I joined them on the *kora*, which involved an arduous hike passing many sacred sites along the way. At one point we had to leap across a deep ravine three times. At another we had to venture out onto a ledge and place the palm of a hand against a particular spot on a cliff face. So many pilgrims had preceded us that the spot on the wall bore the perfect imprint of a human hand, darker than the rock and incredibly smooth to the touch.

About an hour and a half into the walk, nearing the end of the circuit, we climbed up to a high peak where I could see no further way forward. The path ended at a sheer drop, or so it seemed. But then Tenzin led us halfway down the cliff face to a ledge no more than three metres long by one metre wide. When we had all gathered in the same spot, little Sopa started to lower himself, feet first, into a small, dark hole at one end of the ledge.

All I could think to say was 'Bugger'.

Then the lithe frame of Tenzin followed him down into it and soon only Dawa and I were left on the ledge. He gestured that I should go first, either because it was the polite Buddhist thing to do or because he was as concerned as I was about descending into a black hole in the ground. Dawa was no lightweight after all. I looked at the hole, then at Dawa, then back at the hole again. If I went first and got stuck, I would have Dawa to pull me out. Then again, if he could fit through then, surely, so could I.

'After you my friend,' I said, stepping back and giving him a hearty slap on the shoulder.

Dawa dropped to the ground and inched his way into the hole, feet first, then sucked in his ample girth and was soon swallowed whole by the earth. It was like watching a man being devoured by a boa constrictor, bit by bit. Finally, just the top of his head was visible. Then, after one final wriggle, that part of him was gone too.

The snag in my brilliant plan was starkly illuminated under the bright Qinghai sun. I was now alone on a ledge, more than 60 metres down a cliff face, with the only exit at my feet and absolutely no way of knowing what to expect once I was in that tunnel. With no one to say 'go here' or 'go there', I felt a crippling sense of fear. Spawned by doubt, questions started bouncing around in my head. Should I go head first to see what was down there, or feet first like the others? Following the example of the others seemed like the better option. But what if, I wondered, the others were now dead in a heap at the base of the cliff, victims of not being able to see where they were going? I got down on my knees and shouted into the darkness. Seconds later a voice came back, obviously alive, not too stressed, marginally impatient if anything, as if to say, 'Come on, we're waiting'. Relieved to hear their voices, I sat down, swung both feet into the hole and slowly dropped myself in.

It was completely black inside, but I could feel the tunnel wall just a few centimetres from my face. The initial stage was steep and the surface as slippery as ice, worn smooth by the robes of passing pilgrims. Little effort was required to move downwards; in fact, I was continually feeling for something to help slow my progress. I pressed my elbows against the walls and dug my heels into any rocky protrusion I came upon. Finally, the tunnel levelled out a little and I could shuffle along on my back. At one stage a glimmer of light appeared through a 30-centimetre crack in the wall that opened out onto the face of the cliff. Fresh air wafted through, though as I carried on it was soon left behind and the dark returned anew. I sensed the tunnel widening and thought I might be nearing the end, only for my feet to come in contact with a sickening sensation: nothing! No rock, no stone, just air. I had come to a precipice and my legs now dangled over it like noodles hanging from a chopstick. The only thing to do was flip over on my stomach, drop down and hope there was some *terra firma* below. Gripping with my fingernails to slow my descent, I blindly lowered myself and then let out an audible sigh of relief as my right boot reached rock again. Suddenly I could hear Tenzin laughing somewhere below, then a short while later a second voice, rich and mellow, which was Dawa's. Twenty minutes later, having edged my way down and round an unseen bend and over some rougher ground, light appeared between my feet and the tunnel opened out into a small cave about two metres square. At the far end was a crack in the wall about as wide as a man — the source of the light. Never have I been so relieved to see the sun again! And I was happy, too, to see the smirking faces of Tenzin, Sopa and Dawa.

Rite of passage over, it was just a short scramble from here down a wooded slope to the valley bottom. The doors to the temple were open and, having finished the *kora*, the monks were eager to complete their pilgrimage by prostrating themselves before a statue of Buddha. The venerable old man in charge allowed me to enter the inner courtyard and even the shrine itself. It was quiet and eerily dark, and the ceiling seemed not to exist, as if the quilt-wrapped columns on either side of the massive golden Buddha climbed all the way to heaven. Everywhere, on every available surface, there were ornate paintings, carvings or relief sculptures of Buddha. The colours were deep blues, bright reds and golds, with a smattering of white wherever a silk scarf was depicted. A photograph of a smiling Panchen Lama was attached to one of the columns and Tibetan script flowed across the walls. I was invited to follow the monks and prostrate myself before the altar, which I did, copying their actions exactly. Like a holy sacrament, water was then administered to each of us by the old man out of a silver cup. It was a moving experience, to be ushered into such an ancient place and made to feel welcome. The holy shrines of Islam were off limits to non-believers, and I had talked my way into those on the odd occasion. But I did not feel for one minute like an imposter here. Simply, I was a man from the outer world, of computers and corporate ladders, given a brief but uplifting audience with Buddha.

Tenzin and the others were staying on at the temple that night, preparing to spend time meditating in one of the hillside retreats, so I took my leave as the sun began to sink lower and I started upon the long hike back. On the return leg I discovered a possible reason why the boards of the suspension bridge were loose. There were wild dogs in the area, some of whom followed me to the river, so I reversed across the bridge, picking up the boards as I went, creating a gap they had no hope of broaching. Between us ran the river, swift and cold and too deep for them to cross, a moat of safety. We looked at each other across the divide. The largest of the beasts pawed the ground malevolently, drooling into the dust. When I set off again along the other side of the river, they followed me for a while, keeping pace on the opposite bank, then lost interest when the first humble homesteads of Yushu came into view.

TEN

Two Westerners stood by the kerb in the mid-afternoon sun, surrounded by an alien world of horse-drawn carts and burning incense, and talked about the places they had come from. Queensland was home for Danielle, a land of pineapples and ice-cold Castlemaine beer, while Dominique hankered for a fine cheese from his native France. They were both teaching English at Thrangu Monastery, an ancient seat of Buddhist philosophy on the outskirts of Yushu, known in the fourteenth century as the 'Monastery of 1,000 Lamas', until the Mongolian hordes came and killed them all. On hearing about the reason for my journey, they happily invited me up there to take a look around. They were practising Buddhists, and in return for their labours they received spiritual guidance from the monks.

We found a taxi and within half an hour were pulling into the car park beneath the ochre-coloured ramparts of their Tibetan home. Children in red-and-saffron robes ran squealing across a courtyard, chased by an older monk wearing one sandal — the other was being gleefully held aloft by one of the fast-escaping children.

We went up some steps and through a large archway. I was shown into a narrow, walled courtyard set with unpainted doors leading into a variety of rooms. I followed my hosts up a steep wooden staircase to an upstairs level where there were more bedrooms, each with a small window looking out over the valley. The windows were open and the bright yellow curtains wafted in and out in the cool mountain breeze.

Downstairs was the teachers' common room and kitchen, a place where they could escape from the routines of monastic life. It smelt of ash, cooking oil and last night's dinner. A wood stove sat in the middle of the room and an old table was pushed against a window seat, affording anyone seated there a panoramic view of the countryside down below. The room was spartanly furnished, but the overall feeling was warm and cosy.

When news spread of my arrival, we were joined by Scott, Danielle's boyfriend, who was also from Australia.

'You'll stay for a feed?' he asked.

I nodded. 'Anything I can do to help?'

He threw me a can of Chinese beer, which was only slightly cool, and poured some nuts into a bowl. 'Nah mate, you just sit tight and enjoy.'

It was a pleasant way to spend an afternoon. Over my shoulder the valley was changing colour by the minute as the sun went down, while Danielle talked about life at the monastery. The head lama was a 'good bloke' who was away, she said, on business.

'What kind of business does a lama do?' I asked, looking around the room for any sign of a cottage-industry product.

'He attracts wealthy benefactors who give money to help run the whole show here. Right now he's in Taiwan with a billionaire who says she wants to invest.'

'In the building?'

'Well, yes, that and her soul we reckon. Paying for the upkeep of a monastery is one way of making sure your karma is up to scratch.'

Scott laughed in the background. 'Pay now and have a better time in the next life.' He whacked the head off a carrot with a knife the size of a meat cleaver. 'Don't think that's how it works though.'

They were completely open and frank in their appraisal of everything. The monks were good, they said, but could be brutal on the kids if they stepped out of line. I found this surprising, but apparently it was not an uncommon practice in Tibet for monks to discipline children with beatings. Some monks were quicker to strike than others and the teachers tried to make sure the worst offenders were not allowed anywhere near their students. But Danielle and the others couldn't be everywhere all the time.

'It doesn't help that a lot of the monks are not here voluntarily,' she said. 'They are simply the kids their families couldn't care for, or, in the case of a child born with a mental illness, didn't want to care for. They get sent to a monastery for the rest of their lives and they don't have a choice. It's no wonder some of them are screwed up and take it out on the younger ones.'

For a religion based on non-violence, this was a disturbing revelation and at odds with its image of gentleness and harmony.

'There are many good monks too,' added Dominique in a thick French accent. 'Many here in this monastery, and up in the mountains.'

It turned out that way above this monastery was another, smaller retreat. Once those monks who were deemed worthy of selection entered its gates, they could not leave for three years and spent most of that time in meditation. They were cut off, marooned in semi-isolation and allowed only one weekly visitor, who would leave food and supplies outside their gate.

Scott waved a hand in the direction of the hills. 'When we first came here, I hiked into the mountains and found myself high above the building, looking down onto it. I wasn't supposed to be there, so I got out pretty fast, but I saw that these guys had long hair down to their waists.'

A month later, he said, these same monks had completed their time. Their heads were shaved and their clothes stripped away so that they were naked save for a loincloth. Then they sat in a chair while a wet cloth was draped over them. It was a test. In order to become a lama, each monk had to dry the cloth by raising his own body temperature using only the power of meditation.

Night fell and we ate a meal of tofu and vegetables with rice. Afterwards, any remaining scraps were sealed in metal rubbish tins so that the mice and rats couldn't get at them. I asked if they had much of a rodent problem and they all laughed.

'You could say that,' grinned Scott. Then he showed me the gnawed woodwork around the cupboards and some steel mesh over a ventilation hole that was bitten right through. 'But don't let that put you off staying the night.'

We discussed a good many things that evening and much of it related to the lives they had left behind and how their fate had led them to this part of the world. They were just ordinary Australians and a Frenchman, from traditional family backgrounds, who, as Buddhists, had decided they had something to give back to their faith. Teaching was one way they could make a difference and experience a very different kind of life from their own. They weren't missionaries, but simply religious travellers keen to do more than just backpack around the place snapping photographs. I admired them for their conviction and their sense of duty to their fellow human beings. Compared with most other religions I had encountered, Buddhism seemed more likeable and displayed a greater generosity of spirit. Not that the same couldn't be said for adherents of Christianity or Islam, to a degree. It was just that the ordinary humble practitioner of this faith, the common or garden variety of Buddhist, seemed to be on the whole a more affable and caring character.

'Do you feel like a walk tomorrow?' asked Scott. 'Some of the monks are making a pilgrimage to one of the local mountaintops. We could join them.'

'Count me in,' came the voice of Dominique from the next room.

'Me too,' added Danielle.

How could I say no?

The head lama's room was empty, they said, and he wouldn't mind if I bunked down there.

It was a small room beside the kitchen, with just a single bed, a locked wooden chest under the window, and a dresser on which was perched a black-and-white photograph of a monk, who smiled out at me with a radiant benevolence. A silk scarf was draped over one corner of the frame. A pair of sandals sat just inside the door, waiting, like a faithful dog, for their owner to return. I placed my cracked and worn leather boots alongside them. In comparison they appeared massive and outlandish.

When the light from the single bulb in the roof went out and the dogs stopped their barking, I heard the rodents come. The scraping of their claws as they ran across the rafters above my head was like a stampede. Then came the sound of dishes clattering next door. Someone had forgotten to put them away, perhaps, or the invaders were already in the cupboards. I lay still on my bed in the dark, not wanting to see what my mind imagined, an army of rats with their red eyes glinting.

Amazingly, I must have dozed off. But then I woke up smartly when something crawled across my face. I brushed it away, flicked on a torch and there on the floor was an impressively large spider. It moved sedately back towards me, as if stunned. Fearing a repeat of the close encounter, I placed one of my boots gently on top of it and returned to bed. A few hours later, however, when a knock on the door signalled the monks were gathering to start the pilgrimage, I flicked on a torch and found it was squashed flat, a small animal murdered by my own hand — not exactly a very Buddhist thing to do, and in the head lama's bedroom no less. Guiltily, I swept the remains under the bed, and tried to avoid the gaze coming from the photograph on the dresser.

It was pitch black outside in the courtyard when I caught up with the small group, and I could feel the chill of the flagstones coming up through the soles of my walking boots. It wasn't numbingly cold, but cold enough to cause me to wonder if the clothes I had on would be adequate for the possible extremes of temperature at an even higher altitude. But then, as the occasional flash of a penlight illuminated the friendly enquiring figures of the monks around me, providing glimpses of their humble robes and sandals, I decided not to worry. And, as it turned out, the cold was to be the least of the hurdles that day.

We set off in single file, a quartet of monks taking the lead because they possessed the solitary penlight, while the rest of us half trudged, half stumbled in their wake. Danielle had slept in, so it was just Scott, Dominique and me who began to chat as we climbed over a low stone wall and found the bare earth of a rutted mountain track. Not that we were able to talk for long. It soon became blindingly obvious that the pace the monks were setting meant that every breath had to be conserved for one purpose, sucking in oxygen. What made matters worse was not being able to see where we were going. And although the path occasionally evened out, raising our spirits and giving us a chance to recover, it was never long before it would be almost vertical again — a veritable staircase without end.

Scott was the first to go down. We'd been walking for an hour when the sound of his footsteps behind me suddenly halted. I looked back into the darkness and although I couldn't see him I could definitely hear him. Our sole torch was soon brought to bear upon the sad, crumpled form hanging onto a rock and spewing everything he had in his stomach into some bushes.

He raised a hand to shield his eyes from the light: 'S'okay,' he said. 'I'll catch you guys up.'

Dominique was not so sure. He had been brought up in the French Alps near Mont Blanc and knew all too well the first signs of altitude sickness. He offered Scott his water bottle and a handful of nuts, then tried to talk him into going back, but Scott was having none of it. He got back on his feet, wiped the vomit from his chin and carried on walking as if nothing had happened. As he went past he slapped me on the shoulder and said cheerfully, 'See ya at the top.'

Gradually the pre-dawn light made things easier and the going soon became less steep than at the start, though Scott still had to stop periodically to be sick. It must have been rough for him, but he never once looked like quitting, even though every time we came to the crest of one ridge there would be yet another beyond it. By now I could see that the plant life around us was mainly a kind of short brown heather, dotted with dainty alpine flowers in blues and yellows. Rough stones littered the path and would hook any foot not lifted high enough to clear them. The way forward became a war of attrition, with every few steps requiring a pause to recover. My breathing was laboured and my limbs felt like they were filled with lead, yet the monks bounced along, laughing and chatting noisily amongst themselves as if it were a Sunday stroll. They were concerned about Scott, but equally they were worried about making the top in time to see the sunrise, an important part of their ritual. We convinced them to go ahead, and that we would help Scott get through the last few kilometres, something I wasn't a hundred per cent sure we would manage. More and more often he would sit down and then take longer to get going again. At one stage, close to the summit, he even took to crawling.

Eventually, however, we all made it to the top. As the sky turned from pink to blue and the first rays of the sun began to strike the lofty, snow-capped peaks around us, the mountain path ended at the foot of a rocky cairn about two metres high, which was wreathed in innumerable prayer flags that fluttered in the strengthening breeze. It was heavenly, dream-like and ethereal. The colours of the flags, contrasting with the monks' crimson robes and framed by the granite grey of the mountains, were an intoxicating sight. As the light of day started to warm our contented faces, we all stood around grinning at each other, no words being said because none were necessary.

We stayed there a while, contemplating the incredible view, until the monks decided to continue to some other distant mountaintop. For us it was simply a matter of turning around and heading home again. But Scott was starting to show even worse signs of altitude sickness. His speech was slurred and he walked unsteadily. If we didn't get him down soon he might lapse into unconsciousness and have to be carried. Taking an arm each, Dominique and I supported him as we retraced our path to the red-roofed monastery far below. It took forever, and the sun turned from friend to foe as it made the going hot and uncomfortable.

Scott looked as white as a sheet when we eventually got him to a bed. Danielle immediately started to pour liquids into him. The drugs I had on me had no effect and he seemed to be in real trouble. Eventually the decision was made to put him into a car and get him to the local hospital in Yushu as soon as possible. With Scott lying down in the back seat, Danielle in the front and Dominique driving there was no room left for me. I watched them go, the car kicking up an urgent cloud of dust, then followed after on foot until a local farmer came by in a small pick-up truck and took me the rest of the way.

It was a couple of days later that I saw Danielle again in the town. Scott had made a full recovery and was back teaching. I apologised, saying we should have forced him to turn around early that morning, even though he was adamant about continuing, but she clicked her tongue and waved away the apology.

'That boy can be bloody stubborn sometimes,' she said, shaking her head. 'But I reckon I'll keep him.'

* * *

Time was ticking on. I caught up again with Hua and her travelling companions, who had finally managed to repair the damaged wheel on the Jeep. They took me off-road to see a lake, although I suspected it was so Wei could show off the Jeep's 4WD capability. We bumped and trundled our way across sealed and unsealed roads for hours and hours until eventually the shores of Nianjie Cuo came into view. It was beautiful, and the surrounding hills were magnificently reflected in its tranquil waters.

'Here,' announced Wei, 'is the start of the mighty Tongtian River, which flows into the Jinsha River and then into our glorious Yangtze.'

'Actually,' said Hua, unimpressed, 'not exactly.'

'Yes it is!' insisted Wei and he strode off to kick a rock into the water.

Hua smiled cockily and said, 'He hates me.'

To be honest, I told her, we'd come over a hundred kilometres to get to the lake, and there was still the same distance to go on the return leg, so as far as I was concerned Wei could think whatever he liked about the lake, birthplace of the Yangtze or not. But Hua wouldn't drop it. She went on like a worn record about how in school they were taught the many glaciers of the Tibetan plateau were the accepted birthplace of the great rivers of China, not just one location.

'You know a lot, don't you,' I said finally.

'I am very well educated.'

'But can you skip a stone?' I asked.

The Nianjie Cuo may or may not have had much to do with the formation of one of the world's greatest rivers, but it can henceforth lay claim to having been the venue for the greatest stone-skipping competition ever. Wei saw his chance to put the young upstart in her place and, unfortunately for Hua, her stone selection left something to be desired. She'd pick the most unlikely nuggets of rock and watch as they sank almost on impact with the water. Wei's choice of stone was infinitely better and he could get his to skip quite a few times. One particular piece of smooth granite he sent bouncing across the water into the middle of the lake, whereupon it finally ran out of puff and came to a halt, seemingly floating for a split second on the surface. Still wearing his white driving gloves, Wei high-fived everyone in delight. Hua forgot her superiority complex and kissed him on the cheek. The other two men dropped their stones in mock surrender.

In Yushu that night, we celebrated with a few bottles of Qinghai's finest beer and laughed out loud at the idea that stone skipping might soon become an Olympic sport, and Wei its first gold medallist. It was a good way to end a long day.

* * *

After a week had gone by in Yushu, my journal bore a few scribbles in Mandarin and Tibetan, but those merely welcomed me to their country and wished me luck. Mao Tse-tung was not a welcome name either, not amongst the Tibetans anyway. Their ancestors had killed the Communists with impunity, harangued them at every opportunity and driven the Long Marchers back into the mountains where many froze to death. Small wonder then that Mao had returned a decade or so later, to viciously invade the Tibetan homeland and claim it for his own. Mao was never what you might call a forgiving person.

From Yushu there was a road that headed east over the mountains to a place called Garze in Sichuan province, a small town known for its association with the march. It was not a good road, by all accounts, but it was passable, at least until the first winter storms came and closed it for months on end. If I didn't go soon, I'd be trapped, and left with few options except attempting the pass on foot or using some other non-mechanised form of transport. The main difficulty with that idea would be the weeks it would take just getting anywhere. The bus represented an arduous journey in itself, 16 hours at least, depending on landslips along the way. But it was still the fastest route.

The next day I sat in a bus next to a carsick monk who vomited out the window at regular intervals as the countryside rolled by. We were still on a relatively straight road, so it was only going to get worse, I feared. In fact, when we did eventually reach the foothills and the start of the long, slow, winding climb to the first of many passes, he tucked his head down by his ankles and stayed there for four or five hours, seemingly in a state of hibernation. It was like having the whole seat to myself. He was bent so flat and so still, I could have used his back as a table.

In Sershu we stopped to fix a blown tyre. The driver, Gan, rolled the bus onto a kerb, so that the right rear wheel was suspended in the air. Gan was a Muslim, whose religious obligations forced us to stop often so that he could pray. He wore the face of a man devoted to God, and to keeping his bus in one piece. It was a constant battle to maintain it in working order, particularly over such punishing roads as these, but maintain it he did. There was probably not a part of that vehicle he had not, in some way, performed major surgery upon, so much so that I suspected he knew it better than its maker.

In the meantime my carsick monk had unravelled himself and, with a few others, wandered over to a ramshackle building where a middle-aged woman with a stern expression was serving tea from a giant-sized teapot. She was dressed in a long black skirt that dragged on the floor and a red long-sleeved top. Her black hair was plaited down her back and on her head was a white brimmed hat that wouldn't have looked out of place at an English wedding or the Melbourne Cup. Her name was Lolha and she was the self-appointed matriarch of Sershu. Nothing came or went here without Lolha knowing — or passing comment, I assumed — so, not surprisingly, I soon came under her close scrutiny. She tsk-tsked at my unshiny boots and remarked in a Tibetan that needed no translation that I could probably do with a wash. I followed her gaze to my jacket, which still had a few remnants of my travelling companion's first explosive puke on its sleeve. Within minutes it was off my back and being attacked by Lolha with a scrubbing brush in a nearby bucket of water, then hung out to dry in the heat of the Tibetan sun. This was much to the amusement of the others, who joked that Lolha and I were now as good as married. Gan, the driver, who was under the bus but still within earshot, thought it especially funny. He laughed so hard he hit his head on the axle and, when he re-emerged, offered to get my bag down from the luggage rack because clearly I was staying on a bit longer than expected. Meanwhile, Lolha beamed from under the frilly white lace of her wide-brimmed hat.

A well-timed distraction was provided by two young Tibetan men in cowboy hats, who rode up on a Chinese motorbike. They wore matching red coats in the traditional style and manner, with one arm free of its sleeve, which was tied around the waist. They came over and sat themselves down on the stone steps of Lolha's teahouse and chatted noisily with each other. They were in the middle of an argument and seemed to have come to Lolha to settle it. As judge and jury on most things in Sershu, she listened intently to both sides and then gravely delivered her verdict, speaking first to the younger of the two.

'Teshi, you stole your brother's yak?'

'It's not his yak.'

'He is the eldest, so it is his yak and you have to respect that.'

'But he stole my motorbike!'

'Norbu, don't take his motorbike and he won't steal your yak.'

Norbu nodded sombrely in agreement.

'There, that's settled then. Now, you two, I want you to meet my new lover.'

At least that's what I thought she said, because Lolha then gave me the biggest hug. I was slightly relieved when it didn't last too long. Lolha had a wicked sense of humour and enjoyed making people squirm.

It turned out the two young men were her sons and that Lolha had divorced their father many years before. She now had a new partner, I was relieved to hear — although apparently in Tibetan culture it is permissible for a woman to have more than one. Polyandry isn't by any means common; however, it's interesting to note that women in Tibetan culture are not as oppressed as one might imagine, but are quite free, both economically and sexually. They often manage household finances and can own land, which in turn makes divorce easier. Moreover, the Buddhist belief that all of our experiences are constantly changing, and that nothing is permanent, meant that moving on from a relationship was sometimes seen as a healthy thing to do.

Once he got the wheel off, it took Gan a few hours to have it fixed at a garage just down the road, so we had quite a bit of time to relax and hear more of Lolha. The husband she had separated from still lived in the village, but his job took him far away, to where he traded in horses with the Turkic people — sometimes as far west as Xinjiang — so she didn't see him much. Her new partner was his brother, which conveniently made the division of possessions after the divorce simple, given that they all stayed in the same family. I asked her if this happened often and Lolha nodded.

'Why be unhappy?' she shrugged.

I couldn't help but feel this Tibetan view of life made a lot of sense. When separations occurred, those involved did their best to work out a deal whereby houses, land and animals were not split between the parties but were kept together so that the extended family group remained strong. There was no call for expensive lawyers or prolonged legal battles, nor the accompanying hurt that all too often prevailed in Western courtrooms. Here, it was life, and they just got on with it.

Lolha's two sons were big, handsome lads with a keen interest in what lay beyond their town's borders. Whenever they had the chance they'd get up to Yushu or down to Garze, though the latter journey was a lot further and in Garze they had had problems with soldiers in the past.

'What sort of problems?' I asked.

'Teshi got into a fight,' said Norbu, giving his little brother a less-than-friendly clip round the head.

Some soldiers on patrol had stopped Teshi for questioning and pushed him around a little. Teshi's answer had been to go at them with his fists. He was sturdily built but not big enough to take on a whole patrol. They'd given him a broken rib and a night in jail for his trouble.

'Are there soldiers where you come from?' piped up Teshi.

I told him yes, but that our navy was bigger than our army.

'What's a navy?' he asked, and received another clip from his older brother.

'Stupid. A navy is an army on the water.'

'In boats,' I added, just to clarify.

'You live near the sea?' Teshi gasped, looking out at his own horizon.

I told them a story of how, just days before coming to their country, I had been out sailing with my son, Tom. Our ketch, *Tiki*, was an old Peterson 46, an ocean-going vessel built for circumnavigating the world, but this time we were hugging the coastline, heading southeast towards one of the outer islands in Auckland's Hauraki Gulf. The wind was blowing at 15 knots, gusting at 20, a perfect sailing wind creating just a light chop on the water. I'd been telling Tom about Little Mao and the trip, while he grasped the helm and rode out each puff of wind with a skill I hadn't known he possessed.

Suddenly I realised everyone had stopped to listen. They may not have understood all the details, but Lolha, the boys, the other passengers — they were all tuning into this other world that was so unlike their own. But what I also suddenly realised was that this revelation had put up a wall between us. I was an alien, with an alien life, far removed from these concrete steps outside a teahouse on the edge of the Tibetan plateau. The silent pause that lingered afterwards said everything.

After a while, Teshi spoke to his brother.

'I'd like to see the ocean one day,' he said hopefully.

Norbu thought about this for a moment and then playfully grabbed his brother in a headlock.

'Not until you give me back my yak,' he said.

* * *

Young monks at Thrangu Monastery

The vast grasslands of the Tibetan plateau, near Sershu

By the time my jacket had dried in the sun it was time to move on. With a new tyre safely in place, Gan rolled the bus forward off the kerb and motioned for us to climb back on board. Across the road a vast expanse of grassland spread out before us, rolling without a break towards Lhasa, more than 1,000 kilometres distant. Here and there it was dotted with yaks and the ever-present telegraph poles that marched along the roadsides. Buddhism may suggest that life is change and nothing is permanent, but I hoped this pastoral scene would stay just the way it was forever.

On we went to heights that were unmarked by post or sign but were rejoiced in nonetheless by the monks, who crowded around the windows and threw coloured papers out into the cool air, each one printed with a special sutra. Every peak was a celebration. Holy sutras floated on the breeze and littered the ground on the mountain passes in every direction. In a matter of just a few weeks, perhaps, they would be buried in metres of snow. But for now, though an isolated shower or two could be seen in the valleys, it was a clear day. Distant snow-capped peaks glistened majestically. According to my map, some were up to 7,500 metres tall, though they didn't appear so high to the naked eye. It dawned on me that this was because we were viewing them from an already lofty elevation, possibly 4,700 metres, so we were only seeing part of their great bulk. Despite this, they were still impressive, even from a distance. Closer to hand, jagged shards of rock protruded from verdant hillsides, like teeth jutting from a jawbone.

At one stage a young Tibetan started singing in a full and lusty tone, and soon others joined in. Monks put aside their religious chants and began to sing a very different tune, one in which the singer apparently pined for a long-lost sweetheart. We also had one other form of entertainment, which seemed very out of place given the age of the bus: a TV set. Connected to a DVD player under the driver's seat, it played music videos — featuring more males pining for long-lost sweethearts, as the singers walked through fields of wild grasses in full national costume — and a comedy film that had everyone in fits of laughter. It was Chinese and featured a woeful bunch of new army recruits on a madcap adventure that included every slapstick joke in the book. The recruits ran around like idiots, which is probably what the Tibetans loved most about the film — it made the Chinese look stupid.

Sixteen hours and 700 kilometres or so after leaving Yushu, when every bone in my body had been rattled thoroughly and I was on the point of crying 'Enough!', the small town of Garze came into view. Nearby, in 1935, an advance party of soldiers of the Fourth Red Army had quietly passed in the night, speedily making their way towards the neighbouring town of Luding, in order to capture its one and only bridge, so that the rest of the marchers following them could safely cross. As it would have been then, it was dark now, and just a few scattered electric lights shone brightly, no doubt powered by the usual diesel generators. The streets had emptied but, as in most Chinese towns, there was a little place with rooms for rent in the bus station. I took the only room that had a bath and soon sank deep into its tepid embrace. We had been going since 5 a.m. and I smelt of monk puke. A wash was the first thing I needed, followed by a long sleep.

* * *

I was looking at a human thighbone near the water's edge when an explosion came from upstream, a distant booming that reverberated against the mountain walls and made a flock of birds jettison themselves from a nearby tree. A dead fish floated down the river some time later, followed soon after by several more, and then a lot more. All of them upside down in the water.

I was just a few kilometres outside Garze on the Yalong River, which started its journey on the Qinghai plateau and ended over 1,300 kilometres later when it poured into the Yangtze in the very southernmost corner of Sichuan. Most of the houses in Garze were wooden and of a particular two-storey design, and were bunched together in tight little alleyways. Their gates were high and wide, and made from timber with wrought-iron filigree painted red and gold, and they enclosed dusty courtyards filled with chrysanthemums and dahlias of the same two colours.

I had wandered through the village that morning until I found a long swing bridge across the river. At the halfway point, an old woman on a motorbike sped past me in the opposite direction, carrying a load of fresh vegetables in a bamboo backpack. On the far side of the bridge were fields of the same produce in row upon neat row, and a small forest of silver birch ablaze with autumn colours.

The thighbone had caught my attention because of its size. Undoubtedly human, it was evidence of a typical Tibetan Sky burial, where the body is opened up, cut into pieces and fed to vultures, usually high up on a mountain ledge. Gruesome as it may seem, this is simply an effective way of disposing of a body whose spirit, according to Buddhism, has flown; it's also practical, given that wood for cremations is scarce and the ground too hard and stony for digging a grave. But how the thighbone had come to be by the river was a puzzle that I had been pondering when I heard the explosion.

A few kilometres further on, round a bend in the river, I located the source of the destruction. A group of Chinese soldiers were camped amongst a clump of trees and were practising throwing live grenades. As I approached they tossed two more into the river in quick succession and the quiet water erupted. Their beaming smiles softened slightly when they saw me, probably more out of curiosity than fear, although I probably did have a pissed-off look on my face. My Afghan mujahedeen friends of many years ago would have felt the same. They would also have seen the senselessness of detonating live ammunition in the water and not bothering to put a net out. After all, that's how we'd caught fish sometimes, maybe the odd tasty eel if we were lucky. But these guys were just doing it stupidly, for fun. Nevertheless, I greeted them with the kind of respect you reserve for people toting machine guns and they duly responded, inviting me to have a glass of green tea.

They were keeping an eye on the monasteries in the precinct and were part of a much larger company from Changsha, a long way away in Hunan province, Mao's homeland. Apparently there had been some trouble with the monks and I gathered they'd had to knock a few heads together to keep the peace.

It was all pretty normal stuff: regulation, military-standard monk busting. I showed them the passage in my journal, which outlined what I was doing in China, and this received a warm response. The ones who had initially hung back now stepped forward to hear what was written, spoken slowly by one young soldier who stumbled over the longer words. As for an answer to some of the questions concerning the son of Mao, they were less forthcoming. Their average age was probably 19 and none of them had even heard of the young Mao An Hong. It was consistent with most of the reactions I'd had so far. The younger generation was not taught that part of their history, simply because the child was of no consequence. He did not feature in the great and glorious birth of Communism.

However, there was one small ray of sunshine, in the form of the man to my immediate right. He may have been an officer, or at least of a slightly higher rank than the others. He spoke shyly, in broken English, with long gaps between the words as he searched for the correct sentence structure.

'You will go to Changsha?' he asked.

I nodded and said I hoped so, to which he replied, 'Then I must give to you the name of my university history professor. He is very wise.'

The other soldiers were smiling, clearly impressed with our conversation, which made the young man even bolder. He reached into his breast pocket and pulled out a pen and paper. As he wrote the name in English, there were *oohs* and *ahhs* of wonder at this alien alphabet. It wasn't much in the way of a lead, but it was something, a target to aim for. Perhaps in Changsha I would have better luck.

Later that night I celebrated this modest progress at a local restaurant. The small kitchen opened out onto the footpath, casting a spell, with its heavenly aromas, on anyone who walked by. The place was crowded, and I perched on a stool next to a cherubic young Tibetan businessman in a brown leather jacket and his thin young male assistant, who wore a light blue ski jacket. They had finished their meal but, before going, the businessman poured me a glass of tea and insisted on paying for my meal. I asked the woman who ran the kitchen what was on the menu.

'Fish,' she said in a shrill voice.

'Anything else?'

'Only fish today. Lots and lots of fish.'

Taking produce to market across Garze's swing bridge

A proud restaurant owner in Garze

ELEVEN

The bus to Kangding was supposed to arrive early in the morning, but never turned up. The middle-aged Chinese woman in the ticket office, resplendent in a smart blue uniform with gold buttons and a peaked cap, soon tired of the Tibetan passengers' constant demands for information and simply put her window down and left. No one knew what to do. Burdened with large bundles of goods to transport to a distant market, the Tibetans had no other option but to sit and wait — hours, perhaps, maybe days.

With no such luggage in tow, I walked to the edge of Garze and caught a ride with a logging truck headed east. The driver was a short, round man in his forties, with a close-shaved head and a dark mole on his cheek from which sprouted several long, grey hairs. His name was Peng and he was one half of a husband-and-wife transporter tag team. She was asleep behind the curtain that sealed off the back of the cab and her not-so-gentle snoring and occasional flatulent outbursts kept us entertained for hours. Every time she snorted, or let rip with another prodigious fart, we laughed so hard we cried. I learnt that it was his job to drive in one direction and her job to drive in the other; that way they didn't have to talk at all. The perfect marriage, he explained, was based on this simple and enduring principle. Oddly enough, when she did appear much later, she was not the crusty old hag I'd imagined but a quite cherubic woman, who smiled out at me.

We found the missing bus to Kangding later that morning, on its side next to a lorry with the front smashed in. A man in a white shirt was sitting in the shade of the upturned bus, his back against the underside of the vehicle. He waved uncomfortably with his left arm as our truck approached, while his right arm hung limply by his side, but the driver of the logging truck didn't stop. In China, incidents like this one were treated as sideshows put on for the entertainment of others: a car crash attracted interest, particularly if there was blood; a brawl in the street was a welcome break from the tedium of the day. It seemed that the sheer enormity of the country's population — then over 1.3 billion — had robbed everyone of their compassion. Ironically, that indifference could also help some people turn a profit. In Yushu, I had seen a blind man offering punters a glimpse into his empty eye sockets for two yuan a go.

Along the way, villages were few and far between and soon even the black tents of the nomads were nowhere to be seen. The cool air of the Tibetan plateau was gradually being replaced by uncomfortable warmth. Trees became lush and sprang from the banks of fast-flowing rivers that cascaded ever downwards to the waiting Yangtze, the 6,300-kilometre-long river that travelled all the way to the East China Sea. It felt like I was falling from the heavens, tumbling down through endless valleys, where the atmosphere became thick and wet. On and on we journeyed, pausing for food and drink at little roadside kitchens where the smoke from the cooking fires drifted across our path. It was quick and easy fare: noodles in a watery soup, with hot green tea to follow. We sat at small wooden tables on little wooden stools, eating wordlessly.

At one of these humble restaurants I took a walk up the road only a short distance and came to a woman cooking corn over a barrel. A little further on was a large heap of coal in an open-sided bunker of concrete blocks. I was within a few metres of it when, from out of the pile, there suddenly erupted an ugly snarling beast of such canine ferocity I almost fell over backwards. It lunged at me, snapping its chain tight — its jaws would have torn at my throat had those metal links been just a few more in number. The dog stood a metre high at the shoulders and was as black as the coal dust it was covered in. It looked totally evil, like something straight from the pages of a C.S. Lewis or Brothers Grimm tale, with eyes that glowered hideously, hellbent on savagery. Even when I had retreated back down the road, it watched me with a hatred I could not fathom. Only when I was back in the truck and on the road again did I feel my pulse return to normal. I realised, too, that no one had moved a muscle, or said anything to keep the beast in check. Had it broken free, I might have ended up like the man in the shade of the bus to Kangding, a mere lunchtime novelty, torn to pieces for the enjoyment of all.

Peng and his wife were going to Danba, a village near the logging epicentre of Sichuan province. There they would pick up a load of pine and spruce and haul it off to a mill about another day's ride away. Then they would return with the newly milled lumber, all the way back to Yushu, before starting the whole process over again. I asked him what was the hardest thing about his job and he replied that there were three things he battled with the most: blown tyres, broken suspension and earthquakes.

'The first two I can deal with,' Peng said. 'But when mountains fall down and bury the roads, I can do nothing but sit and wait.'

He then went on to describe an incident a few years earlier when he and his wife had narrowly missed being taken out by a landslide that engulfed the road in front of and behind them. Marooned until help came, they had built a shelter using the timber in the truck and set up house on the road. They had remained there for two weeks, living off rainwater and berries, and an occasional bit of roast meat provided by the birds the man shot with his rifle.

'You carry a gun?' I asked, looking about the empty cab.

With his free hand Peng reached through the curtain and squeezed the leg of his wife, who let out a shriek. She rolled to one side to allow him to search under the bedding, from where he produced a fine but quite ancient looking bolt-action rifle. I recognised it as Russian, from its markings and because I'd seen one like it before in Afghanistan. The Soviet Mosin–Nagant is famous all round the world. Today it is mostly found in the hands of gun collectors, but in the 1930s it was the trusted friend of every single Russian soldier. Over 37 million were eventually produced and no doubt quite a proportion found their way across the border into China, destined for Mao's Communist troops. Although there was little concrete evidence that showed the Soviets had supplied Mao with anything other than hard cash, this was clearly some kind of proof that they had, on occasion, offered something more.

'You shoot?' he asked, passing it to me casually as he kept one eye on the road. I nodded and then wondered what I'd let myself in for when moments later he pulled over on a deserted stretch of road and started ferreting around in the back for some ammunition. He located a small cardboard box and loaded the magazine with five rounds. Then we took turns at putting holes in a plastic drink bottle he had tied to a tree, the boom of the gunfire fortunately scaring off anything living nearby. When we finished, the air was heavy with the smell of cordite and a primeval sense of satisfaction. The man told me he'd won the rifle in a fight, but something told me this was more bravado than truth. Still, it was fascinating to think this old piece of Communist military history might have once belonged to a soldier on the Long March.

A few kilometres further on, the couple turned off to Danba. They dropped me at the junction, where I sat on a tree stump and waited for another ride to take me the rest of the way to Kangding. I didn't have long to wait. When a Volkswagen Passat police car came roaring up with its lights flashing, I thought this was turning out to be quite a day.

The car stopped abruptly in a cloud of dust, as if I was the person its passengers were looking for. I felt complicit in some crime, and began wondering if shooting live rounds in the forest had been such a great idea. Happily, though, it was just a lift they were offering and I didn't think twice about accepting a seat in the back — after all, what harm could come from riding with the local constabulary?

They were two senior policemen, in their middle age, and, despite their obvious haste, still had time to exchange pleasantries in broken English.

'Where you from?'

'How long you stay in China?'

'Where you go?'

We barrelled along a dirt road at breakneck speed. I checked for a seatbelt but couldn't find one on my side by the window. There was a lap belt in the middle, however, so I sat there and strapped myself in. Rows of poplar trees flashed by like picket fences until we came across a team of labourers who had been pouring concrete to make a new road in the middle of nowhere. Big, burly men, they were covered in fine white dust, which made them look like ghosts. As we approached, they were standing in front of a tin shed, smoking.

The driver stopped the car and motioned for me to stay put. Then he and his partner climbed out, straightened themselves as if after a long drive, and hitched up their trousers. As they walked over to the group they nonchalantly unclipped their pistol holsters. There ensued a brief discussion, during which the workers seemed to be explaining what was inside the tin shed. It was now rocking from side to side and from within it I could hear a loud voice shouting fiercely.

Then the men stamped out their cigarettes and rolled up their sleeves, forming a semi-circle round the shed door. Someone must have opened it at this point because out tumbled a large figure, who was almost immediately wrestled to the ground by the workers. In jumped one of the policemen with a pair of handcuffs and, when the group parted again, he was helping a tall, very red faced man with his hands bound behind his back to his feet and pushing him towards the car.

Minutes later, I was sharing the back seat with a man who had, according to the police, gone nuts that morning and almost killed someone with a shovel. His name was Gu, or Crazy Gu as the policemen laughingly referred to him, clearly not without some justification.

'I'll stomp on your stinking face, damn you! I've done nothing to deserve being treated like this,' he roared. Then he started bellowing like a bull for no apparent reason.

Fortunately, Crazy Gu was a thirsty man from having been shut in a tin shed all day, so when I offered to share the contents of my water bottle with him he started to calm down. At least for the time being, the bellowing stopped.

Based on what the policemen told me, and what I could get out of Gu himself, I was then able to piece together the story of his unhappiness. The stretch of road that he had been working on for the past six months was 125 kilometres long and crossed very difficult terrain. The road-making company paid him a pittance, barely enough to send home to his wife and family. He had not seen them at all in this time, although his wife wrote to him every week. Then during the past month he had received no letters and no money. The company had withheld both because they said Gu was not working fast enough; they'd said he was lazy — 125 kilometres of roadway in six months was not enough, apparently — and the punishment was laid down in order to make Gu pick up the pace of construction. But, unfortunately for his foreman, the only thing Gu decided to pick up was the wooden handle of the nearest spade. He'd knocked the man completely senseless and was now going to pay the price.

Gu may have been mad, but he'd been driven that way by the strain of his labours and by the deprivation of news from home. There was no such thing as a union in this part of the world, and what the company felt like doing, the company did. Resistance was futile, for although Gu was a strong man, he was no match for a group of faceless managers in some far-flung head office. I watched him gaze out the window, occasionally struggling with the handcuffs that bound him. What he was thinking about I had no way of knowing. His own fate perhaps, or that of his family, now deprived of an income? Or was it that he was glad to be finally free of that boring stretch of concrete road, with over a hundred kilometres behind him but still hundreds more to go. Even a month in jail might be better than that. I thought then about the road sweepers I'd seen on the long, empty roads of the Qinghai plateau. In the middle of those vast expanses, there they would be, slowly working their way along an eternity of bitumen with a straw broom. It would take a special mind to deal with that kind of job, a mind that could switch off and live with the fact that each day, each kilometre, each minute would be the same as the last. You'd need the mental fortitude of a marathon runner and the patience of a monk. I certainly couldn't do it, and clearly these were qualities Gu did not possess either — he certainly didn't look anything like a marathon runner or a monk.

The sunlight through the trees played upon his face as we hurtled along, and his eyelids grew heavy. After a while, he was asleep, breathing peacefully, eyes moving silently behind their lids, softly dreaming.

***

In Kangding, an ancient trading town nestled deep within the confluence of three valleys and surrounded on all sides by bare mountainsides, the policemen dropped me off at a public square that was packed with people playing badminton. It was said that some of the Long Marchers who made it this far had stayed behind here, in order to defend the rear. If so, and they survived, then here, possibly, were their descendants, athletically involved in the pursuit of a shuttlecock.

The air was filled with the swish of racquets and a rumbling sound like a constant landslide, which turned out to be a river coursing its way, via deep concrete channels, around the buildings. These were mostly multistoreyed, ugly concrete blocks that looked like they'd been put up in a hurry. Bits of them still needed finishing. Gutters hung at strange angles so that water dripped from them onto the streets below. Here and there the white plaster that clung to the architecture had cracked and fallen away, lying in heaps on the ground. People took no notice and walked around them as if they weren't there. It wasn't until later that I found out that Kangding was well known for its earthquakes and that everyone had long since given up patching over the cracks. I asked one man if the newer buildings were earthquake-proof and he simply shook his head. The town planners, however, clearly loved their badminton and had poured money into keeping everyone busy in this way, perhaps to stop them thinking about earthquakes.

As always, given that this was a long, long way from the more popular tourist sites of China, my arrival was greeted

A monk checks a prayer room at Kumbum Monastery

High up in Garze, with the valley spread out below

Lola's boys, arguing over a stolen yak in Sershu

Instead of goods, old men trade stories at Yushu's market

Under a painting of the Long March, passengers wait for a bus at Jinggangshan

In Moxi, chillis and corn dry in the sun

A roadside stall sells food for weary travellers in Sichuan province

Students in Ruijin grab a nap between classes

Playing *jianzi*, a Chinese form of Hacky Sack

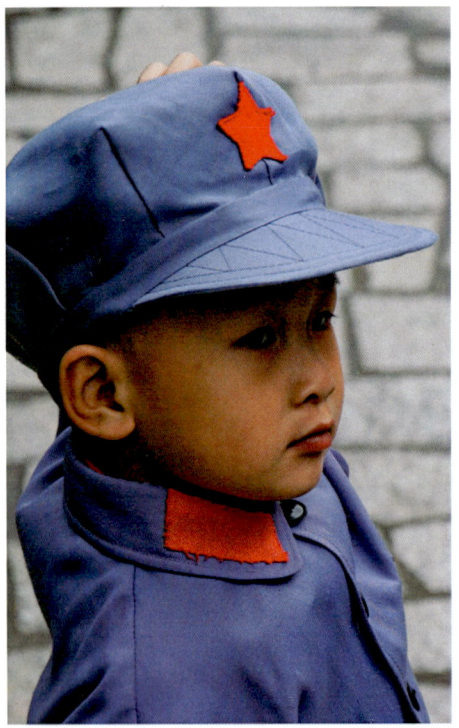

A young 'Red Traveller' in Jinggangshan

Off to the chopping block to prepare a meal

Mist shrouds the high peaks of Jinggangshan

An elderly woman living on her own, near Yudu

Sitting outside, watching the world go by, in Ruijin

with great interest. I was offered a place on a wooden bench from which to watch the badminton and given tea from a large red thermos by a group of elderly women. They fussed over my jacket that was torn at the shoulder and soon found a needle and thread to effect a repair. Then a badminton racquet was offered to me. Although tennis is my natural game, I'd inherited my father's ability to pick up any bat or ball and play with it like it was second nature. I was able to hold my own against my first opponent, and then win. Stiffer opposition was found in a youngster in a light blue Adidas tracksuit, but he too was despatched with relative ease. Suddenly I found myself promoted to the next grade up, on centre court. Someone carried my bag to the sideline. My next opponent was a fit young man in his twenties, named Chan. He looked nervous at the prospect of potentially losing to a foreigner. National pride was at stake, bets were being made within earshot. The roar of the river and that of the growing crowd created an impromptu grand-final atmosphere at 2,500 metres. I stripped off my recently repaired jacket and played with all the athleticism I could muster, but I lost in a grippingly close encounter in which both players had multiple match points.

Chan sank to his knees when my final shot went wide, no doubt relieved he had avoided embarrassment in front of his home crowd, and then jumped up to shake my outstretched hand. Despite the result, I'd won a new friend. He was shorter than me by several centimetres, but, as I'd already found out, his lithe frame possessed the speed and agility of an antelope. I felt like Goliath having been bettered by David's slingshot.

When Chan took me to his family home I noticed a well-stocked trophy cabinet in the corner of the main room. In most Chinese homes this position would have been reserved for a television or an air conditioner, but not in Chan's. Clearly, he was quite an athlete. I asked if all the trophies were for badminton and he said no then dropped into a half-crouch table-tennis position and expertly sent an imaginary ping-pong ball rocketing across the room. Chan told me he had won at county level but that China was overflowing with top-quality table-tennis players and so he'd placed his hopes of a sporting career in badminton.

'Are you champion in your country?' he asked.

Not wanting to make too great a point about how he'd only narrowly beaten someone who hadn't hit a shuttlecock since high school, I nodded in reply, and so found myself admitted somewhat uncomfortably into the world of Australasia's badminton elite.

Chan, along with his mother, father and grandfather, lived in a two-room apartment in the older section of Kangding. His grandfather remembered the great earthquake of 1955, when the hillsides fell down upon them in great waves of earth, and boulders the size of houses rolled through the town, smashing to matchsticks anything that stood in their way. The Communists built new homes out of concrete and these he trusted would fare better in such circumstances.

'Stone against wood is no contest. But stone against stone is another matter,' translated Chan.

Located close to the Tibetan plateau, Kangding had been a major trading place for centuries. In the old days, Chinese porters or 'coolies' would arrive with blocks of compressed tea leaves on their backs to trade for Tibetan wool. These 'tea bricks' were not only a source of food and drink, but also a currency. Tibetans trusted in tea bricks more than a piece of metal and for good reason: in times of hardship you couldn't eat iron, but you could consume the tea by mixing it with water and barley flour.

Back in London in the 1990s when I used to frequent the Royal Geographical Society, I came across the journals and photographs of a fellow by the name of Ernest Henry Wilson, from Chipping Campden in Gloucestershire. His occupation in 1902 was listed as 'plant collector' and he was one of the first Westerners to travel far and wide in the Chinese interior, gathering hundreds of plant species and giving them names, occasionally his own. There are many species of plant life he inflicted with the name 'Wilson', though the humble 'tea brick' was not one of them. But it was through his black-and-white photographs of porters carrying huge loads of these 'bricks' that their existence was first brought to the attention of Victorian England.

He was an intrepid explorer, so much so that when an earthquake caused an avalanche that broke his femur, he used a leg of his camera tripod as a splint while he was carried for three days to civilisation. Wilson died in a car accident in Massachusetts in 1930, but you can trace his legacy in a great many garden stores today.

Chan's mother was an excellent cook and ran a small eating house on the ground floor of their apartment building. We went down there for some Sichuan specialities like chilli hot pot and spicy deep-fried rabbit, after which everyone had a good laugh when my mouth went numb from all the Sichuan pepper. It was intensely fragrant and tasted of citrus, but it made my tongue feel like I'd been sucking on a battery terminal.

'You like hot pot?' teased Chan.

'Yeth,' I said. 'Very nithe.'

Other than earthquakes, if there is one thing Sichuan is famous for, it's spicy food. The locals gobble chillies like chocolate, but fortunately they have the good sense to prepare 'cooling' dishes as well. One of these is tea-smoked duck, simply because it contains relatively few spices. Chan's mother had marinated the duck for some hours, then smoked it over tea leaves and camphor twigs, before steaming and then deep-frying it so that it turned crisp. Because it takes so long to prepare, this dish is made only rarely, but my timing was excellent: today was tea-smoked duck day.

After gorging myself on all this wonderful food, I tried to pay, but my offer was, once again, generously turned down. So I thought I would at least try to leave them with a present of sorts. I'd noticed Chan's grandfather complaining of swollen ankles and feet, so the next day I found a department store that sold China's latest invention, 'The Huawei Heavenly Foot Bath'. It had been advertised on all the buses throughout Qinghai province. I couldn't be sure of its efficacy, but it was, I hoped, the thought that would count. As it turned out, when I turned up on his doorstep the next day with the box under my arm, Chan's grandfather couldn't have been more pleased.

'My grandfather says, every time he bathes his feet, he will think of you,' Chan said.

It was an honour I was entirely happy to accept.

* * *

I was unsettled in Kangding, perhaps because no one would answer any questions I had relating to Mao, the march or anything else that could be deemed to be politically sensitive. I stayed only one day more before boarding a bus to Luding to view its famous bridge. On the day of my departure I learnt that an official visit from a junior Minister of Sport and Tourism, no less, was soon to be announced. That went a long way to explaining why so many were out and about, throwing themselves into every sporting endeavour. It also explained why they were so mute on the subject of Mao. I hoped that Luding was not expecting a similar visitation.

The official story of Luding Bridge recounts that, in 1935, under a hail of gunfire, a small group of Mao's finest soldiers from the Fourth Army crawled across the bridge and subdued the enemy on the other side, saving thousands of lives. It's a pivotal moment in Communist history and much glorified by the media; as a result, it draws hordes of China's Red Travellers to Luding, who swarm through the town buying cheap Mao memorabilia for their trophy cabinets. 'Red Traveller' is a term the Chinese bestow upon themselves. Like the term 'haji', which Muslims often add to their names once they have made the pilgrimage to Mecca, it is an honorific title. To become a Red Traveller you must pinpoint the key places in Communist history and make your pilgrimage to them — places like Luding. It is a rite of passage for every good and faithful Communist Party member, to prove their devotion to the Great Helmsman and his teachings.

I spoke to the woman at the Luding Bridge information desk and asked her for details on the battle. But before answering my question she asked, beaming with self-importance and pride in her own linguistic ability, what language I required it in.

'English,' I said in English.

'Are you sure?' she replied.

'I'm sure. Why?'

'Because the German version is longer and there is a song.'

With that, she started to sing a song in German about the Battle of Luding Bridge. It had been translated from the original Chinese by Otto Braun, a German Communist who was a military advisor to Mao in the 1930s. Otto was actually a spy, making sure the Soviets weren't the only ones with a hand to play in the formation of a Communist China. He went with Mao on the Long March, was known by the Chinese name Li De and took a Chinese wife, though apparently she had to be ordered to marry him — Chinese women were wary of foreigners and considered them unclean. Perhaps because there was little in the way of romance in his life, Otto sought a creative outlet in composing military ballads.

'English will be fine,' I said to the woman, and she then recited the story from memory:

'The Luding Bridge was built many centuries ago, made with heavy iron chains that stretched across the river. On each side the ends were embedded under great piles of rock, while thick wooden boards were lashed over the chains to make the road of the bridge. However,' she said, raising a finger in the air for dramatic effect, 'upon their arrival the brave men and women of the Red Army found the boards on their side were missing, leaving only the bare iron chains swinging across the chasm.

'Down below, the river waters ran fast and furious, breaking with unimaginable force against the boulders that rose from the riverbed. White foam flew high into the air and the roar of the rushing torrent was deafening. Not even a fish could swim against that water. Crossing by boat was out of the question. The bridge had to be taken, but on the opposite bank, with a regiment of troops in support, an enemy machine gun waited for them. The Sichuanese never imagined the Reds would try to cross using the chains alone. It was madness. But the Reds were desperate and, one by one, 30 Red soldiers stepped forward to risk their lives.

'The attack began at four in the afternoon. Together, the Red Army buglers blew the charge and every weapon the Reds possessed was fired at the enemy positions. Carrying Tommy guns and knives strapped to their backs, with a dozen grenades apiece tucked into their belts, the Red heroes, led by Commander Liao, climbed across the swaying chains into a storm of bullets. Behind them came the officers and men of 3rd Company, each carrying a thick wooden plank. With each plank, though, they paid a heavy price.

'Snipers shot at the Reds climbing high above the water. The first hero was hit, and fell to his death in the current below, then a second, and a third. But when one was killed, another warrior stepped up to take his place. Never before had the Sichuanese enemy seen such bravery — men and boys ready to give up their lives to ensure the safety of their comrades. But each board that was laid down gave protection to the Reds and so, little by little, they came nearer. The enemy bullets began to bounce off the planking and the Sichuanese grew fearful.

'At last, one Red crawled up over the bridge flooring and tossed a grenade with perfect aim into the enemy redoubt. The enemy Nationalist officers ordered their soldiers to tear up the rest of the planking, but it was too late. Instead they set them on fire with kerosene, though even this did not hold back our heroes. The Reds crawled forward on their hands and knees through the flames, tossing grenade after grenade into the enemy machine-gun nest, until the Nationalist guns were silent and their soldiers had fled.

'A handful of men gave their lives that day, many others were burnt and wounded, so that thousands of their comrades could cross the bridge over the treacherous Dadu River and escape to safety. By the time the Nationalist reinforcements arrived, the Red Army had vanished into the mountains.

'Did you like it?' she asked finally, taking a sip from a mug of tea that was kept hot by a ceramic lid decorated with red dragons.

'Amazing,' I replied, though it was more her ability to remember it all so well that impressed me.

Otherwise, the most interesting thing about the story was the way the Communists had fabricated such a gargantuan lie around the capture of this insignificant bridge. From my research I knew the truth to be far less dramatic, something that was confirmed to me later by an elderly, slightly stooped man I met on the footpath by the river. He carried a wooden cane which he tapped on the ground as he walked, as if he were on ice and was unsure of its thickness. When I came close he stopped, straightened himself and greeted me curiously, interested to know who I was. His face lit up when I answered and there came a flurry of the usual questions, which I was well used to by now. It was quite some time before I managed to ask a question of my own — whether he knew anything about the bridge's history, for example. Quite proudly, he explained how his father had witnessed the crossing. The Red Army had simply arrived one day and crossed the bridge without incident, watched by the local inhabitants, who took pity on the bedraggled columns of soldiers and offered them rice and water. No shots were fired and not a single casualty was suffered, amongst the soldiers or the villagers. The only losses were the stores of food the Red Army confiscated when they departed a few days later.

'They took my father's pigs,' he muttered sadly, looking into the distance over my shoulder, 'and paid nothing for them in return.'

He zipped up his dark green padded jacket and hugged himself, shivering slightly in the cool breeze that had suddenly enveloped us.

'Winter is coming,' he said. 'Where will you sleep tonight?'

I told him I didn't have a place in mind. I had arrived at the station and put my old army kitbag in storage. There was nothing in it I needed. Everything of importance — camera, toothbrush, soap, passport, journals and money — I had with me in a shoulder bag.

'Then come with me,' he said.

He took my arm and we walked side by side a short distance to a panelled gate painted in reds and yellows that stood head-high between two houses. With an arthritic hand he reached through a hole in the gate and fumbled with a latch until the gate opened, revealing a series of shallow steps that descended towards and ended abruptly at the river. In a small eddy of water, and tied by a stout rope to a wooden post in a rock, nestled a wooden, clinker-built rowboat.

'Get in,' he said, gesturing in the general direction of the vessel. I looked at the fast-flowing river and wondered how safe it was, but the old man seemed not to have any concerns at all. It was as if this was as mundane a daily chore as putting out the cat or collecting the mail. So I stepped into the middle of the boat, sat down on a wooden seat and waited as the old man took his place at the stern. There was a short tiller attached to a rudder that he gripped tightly with the bony fingers of his right hand.

'Now,' he announced, 'pull the rope.'

I examined the heavy line that was tied to the bow, and which then disappeared into the murky green river water in front of us. Obediently I tugged at it, raising it out of the water slightly and then held on as our little vessel edged forward. I assumed there would be further instructions. After all, there were no oars, so it seemed to me there must be some mystery form of propulsion yet to be revealed, otherwise we'd be at the mercy of the current, save for what steerage the little rudder might provide. But there were no further orders. The old man merely untied the remaining line that anchored us to the little dock and let it go.

Instantly we were picked up by the flow of water and swept away from the bank, out towards the middle. I held on with grim determination to the line and, as the tension came on, it lifted even more from the water, revealing that it was tied to the opposite bank, 100 metres upstream. With the old man steering us in the same direction and the current pushing us there as well, we sped sideways across the river. Within another 30 seconds we had safely crossed and were edging closer to the opposite bank, where another set of stone steps awaited. With a soft thud the rowboat bumped against them, the motion of the water holding us in place as I found another length of cord to secure our vessel more permanently. I clambered out and stood on the steps, looking back at the place we had come from, a good 40 or so metres away. The old man had effectively 'swung' the boat across the river like a pendulum. If that wasn't miraculous enough, as he gripped the handrail and mounted each stone step one at a time, I realised suddenly that it wasn't just old age he had to deal with, it was his lack of sight. He was almost completely blind, which explained a number of things: the cane stick, the way he often looked off into the distance or down at the ground when talking — which I had simply taken as the eccentric habits of an elderly Chinese gent — and the way he held my arm as we walked. All these hurdles he seemed to just take in his stride, never complaining about the difficulties that might have tried the patience of much younger, sighted people.

I followed him up the steps until we came to another doorway painted in the same bright colours as the one on the other side. This one creaked open on rusty hinges and soon we were standing in a cobbled stone alleyway between two houses, both two-storeyed and made of vertical planks of a dark timber that was papered here and there with faded posters advertising old DVD movies. Above our heads were shuttered windows and from one I could hear a kitten mewing. Two middle-aged women sat on some stone steps outside a wide doorway and they smiled and nodded as we passed between them to go inside. It was dark, and for a moment I was the one holding onto the old man's arm as my eyes adjusted. Fortunately we soon came to an internal courtyard that was open to the grey sky and I could take in the surroundings more easily.

The courtyard was about 10 metres square and its floor was laid with the same cobblestones as those in the alleyway. It looked clean and recently swept. At the centre was a deep well that was sheer-sided, except for small brick extrusions every foot or so that could be used as a ladder by the very nimble. Nearby was a red plastic bucket tied to a length of rope; when the old man's cane touched it, he raised his voice in anger and called for its immediate removal. One of the ladies from the front steps appeared, hurriedly picked it up and dropped it halfway down the shaft, before securing the rope to an iron ring on the lip of the well. Hearing this, the old man grunted and we shuffled over to some seats against the courtyard wall. There were several wooden doors around the perimeter, all firmly shut, that looked well used and slightly askew. I asked where they went and he said this was where his family members lived. He had a grandson who was married and lived with him in the apartment directly opposite us. His grandson's wife's family lived behind the door on the right, and the corner door to our left led to a spare room that he said I could sleep in for the equivalent of a few dollars.

'I will get them,' he whispered, nodding towards the women, 'to remove the goat.'

Chinese tourists stare in awe at the Luding Bridge

The entrance to old man Hsu's house, Luding

With that, he barked out some more commands and in due course the goat was led from where it had obviously taken up residence and was then shackled to the iron ring on the well, where it remained for the rest of the day, forlornly chewing on the husks of a dried corn cob.

The old man's name was Hsu Teh-Huai. He was 72½ — a good age, he noted, smiling — and had been a teacher all his life, even through the Cultural Revolution, when the Communists had persecuted teachers and sent many, including him, onto the land to work. He had never given up his classes though. He simply moved them from the schoolroom to the outdoors, where he taught physics and chemistry amongst fields of barley and rice. Eventually the Communists let him go back to the school in order to lecture on Party-approved subjects — he didn't say what, but judging from the smirk on his face he must have ignored those orders and continued with his own syllabus.

'Do you like science?' he enquired.

'Yes,' I replied.

He nodded, then tapped at the ground with his cane. 'It is real and solid, like this stone. You can stand on it, build on it. The Communists would have me teach lies instead, and you can't build anything of substance on those.'

Under Mao in the 1960s, anyone who didn't rebel alongside the Red Army was labelled a 'rightist' and such people were often sent away for re-education, or simply shot. As with many revolutions, it was the young intelligentsia, fresh from their universities in the big cities who became the most ardent supporters, calling themselves the 'Red Guards' and spouting forth slogans and political rhetoric that it was risky to ignore, and downright dangerous to disobey. They were organised, their numbers were in the millions and growing by the day, and in some cases they were armed with more than just righteousness. They were a militant mob, hellbent on ridding their world of any perceived threat to their leader, Mao Tse-tung. Often those who were singled out for punishment were prominent writers, artists, scholars and other professionals such as doctors and teachers.

I asked Hsu if he had suffered during this period, and he held out the little finger of his left hand. Most of it was missing, chopped off, he said, by a young man who accused Hsu of being privileged and 'bourgeois'.

'I don't think he knew the meaning of the word,' he said, somewhat bitterly.

I looked at Hsu's clothes and saw the careful needlework repairs that kept sleeve attached to shoulder and pocket connected to breast. There was nothing 'bourgeois' about him at all. Far from it: judging from the roughness of his hands, he had clearly been no stranger to hard work through the years.

'Of course,' he added a few moments later, absent-mindedly rubbing the stump of his little finger, 'I had to give up playing the organ.'

He went on to describe a love of French classical music, principally Claude Debussy and Maurice Ravel, the early musical impressionists, and later he would show me an old vinyl recording of Debussy's *String Quartet in G Minor*. His gramophone player no longer worked, but he kept the treasured record nonetheless. It had come from a Catholic missionary in the 1950s, as had the pipe organ that he had played at the missionary's home in a nearby village. I asked him what had happened to the organ but he didn't know.

'Red Guards took it. Maybe it was broken up and used for firewood,' he said wistfully. 'During the Revolution the winters were very long and cold.'

By now, the light of day was fading and the temperature in the courtyard had suddenly dropped, causing Hsu to shiver. It was like a chill had risen up from the well and now flowed over our feet. Old man Hsu took me inside his home to where a young woman stood by a wooden chopping block, cleaver in hand as she prepared the evening meal. In my honour Hsu had ordered a chicken to be killed and a special stew made from it called *yin-guo,* after the ginkgo berries that are its main ingredient. He said the berries would make me strong for my journey ahead.

'Do you know,' he asked, 'that the only trees to survive the blast at Hiroshima were ginkgos? They are still alive today, only a kilometre from where the bomb exploded.'

It was dark when we sat down to eat in a small, wood-panelled room off the kitchen, five of us on wooden stools round a Formica-topped table covered in a plastic mat. It was printed with a picture of a mountain valley in autumn, a scene of pastoral calm and tranquillity. With us were Hsu's grandson and granddaughter-in-law, and the young cook, who still wore her white apron. We slurped our soups noisily, in classic Chinese style, and talked about politics and music. Much to Hsu's dismay, his granddaughter-in-law was more interested in the Backstreet Boys than Debussy, and so the conversation excluded him while she sought to find out more about the American super-band. I proved something of a disappointment, however, admitting that I didn't know the title of their comeback album. In fact, I didn't even know they had split up. Apparently, this was like being unaware that the world had stopped turning. Despite this inexcusable ignorance, she said that at least my presence gave her a chance to practise the English she'd learnt in school. Strangely, her accent was southern-states American, the result of her teacher having lived much of his life in Texas. At regular intervals — usually whenever I didn't know something about her favourite boy band — she exclaimed, 'Oh my gawsh!'

Down the other end of the table, Hsu was dropping off to sleep and soon the young cook rose quietly and guided him from the room. The grandson, who hadn't said a word all evening, let out a yawn. I suddenly realised that all their beds were in the room we were eating in; by staying up I was keeping everyone awake. So I made my excuses and also retired for the night. They gave me a torch and I walked past the goat, still tied to the well, and entered the room allocated to me. Inside was a freshly made bed near a single window that afforded a glimpse of dark water rushing by below. The moon was up and, although not full, its light filled the room, illuminating another door against which someone had pushed the bed. It was locked, but the key was on the window ledge and, although the lock was old, it turned eventually. The door opened inwards to reveal a small windowless room that smelt of hay and goat. The beam of my torch fell upon dusty farmyard equipment, a collection of plastic buckets and, in the corner, partially covered by several layers of sackcloth, a small piece of an old man's life, in the form of a 21-pipe organ.

Exactly why Hsu had decided not to tell me the truth regarding the instrument was anyone's guess. Everyone has their secrets after all, the things that really make us who we are, as opposed to those parts of us we choose to have on public display. Perhaps his story of it being broken up for firewood might have been more allegorical, alluding to his hands being busted by the Red Guards, rather than the organ itself.

As I lay on the bed and listened to the wooden house creaking as it cooled down, sinking onto its piles like an old man easing himself into an armchair, I thought about my old man — the one I was looking for, Mao An Hong, son of Mao Senior. If alive, was he doing just that somewhere? Slowly resting his bones for the night, with his own secrets kept safe about him — secrets that, if at all possible, I fully intended to uncover? Was it right or wrong to try to do that? Hsu would not have liked his guest prying into places he was not supposed to see; he would have considered that rude and disrespectful. And yet that was exactly what I was doing: poking around in the dark for some kind of answer to a timeless riddle.

✻ ✻ ✻

In the morning I was on the road again, this time to Moxi, another sleepy township deep in the wooded mountains that had seen the passing of Mao and his massive entourage of Long Marchers, including a still-grieving He Zizhen.

Under the vaulted roof of an old Catholic church festooned with pink and yellow flowers, I cornered two old ladies and tried to extract some information about what had happened here during the Long March, but despite my repeated questions they would only smile and echo the same apology over and over: 'Bù zhīdào, bù zhīdào,' — I don't know, I don't know.

I suspected the problem was not just that they didn't know anything, but that here in the Mao tourist belt I was meeting people (old man Hsu aside) who were groomed to recite a textbook version of events and nothing else. It was maddening to say the least, but not entirely unexpected. The glorification of Mao was always going to be part theatre, part circus. Every house he had been in, every well he had drunk from was sacred ground. In some instances the government authorities had even constructed sites and attached stories to them: 'On this hilltop fort Mao addressed the Red Army before a battle', or 'In this room Mao composed a stirring poem that filled the hearts of his followers with love'. In Moxi, at least the buildings were authentic and, indeed, Mao *had* stayed here, if only for a few nights to meet with his commanders and plot the next phase of the march.

Beside the church was the house he had slept in, a 1920s stone and timber house with a sweeping tiled roof, each corner of which was turned up like the toe of an Arabian slipper. An elderly guard sat asleep on the front veranda beside a small wooden table that was bare except for an empty teacup and a book of tickets. I cleared my throat but he didn't wake. The dusty floorboards creaked as I went up a flight of stairs to the dimly lit, sparsely furnished rooms on the second floor. In one, a wooden bed stood in a corner; beneath the only window were a heavy wooden chair and a writing desk. A portrait of the young Mao in uniform looked down from a roughly plastered wall. At the other end of the hallway was a similar room, containing only a rustic wooden table and bench seats under a single, bare light bulb.

I imagined Mao and a few of his fellow leaders — the sly military tactician Zhu De, one of the original leaders of the Communist Party who had defected to Mao with 10,000 of his troops in 1928, and the highly ambitious and mercurial Lin Biao, another defector from the forces of Chiang Kai-shek — seated across the table from each other, deep in conversation about the Nationalist army hot on their trail. It felt as if they had just left the room only moments earlier.

Perhaps it was here Zhu De had devised the four military slogans that helped bring order to the sometimes-ragtag Red Army. Before defecting to the Communists, Zhu was used to the highly trained officers and soldiers he commanded in Chiang Kai-shek's more disciplined regiments. He would have had no time for disorder or disarray, so he had come up with the pillars of partisan warfare on which the Red Army successfully grew. They were incredibly simple:

When the enemy advances, we retreat.
When the enemy halts and encamps, we trouble them.
When the enemy seeks to avoid a battle, we attack.
When the enemy retreats, we pursue.

Of these two men, however, Lin Biao was possibly the more interesting. Secretly, he was known to criticise Mao, believing him to be more in love with himself than the Party. But in public Lin Biao was an outspoken advocate of everything Mao — what he said, what he thought and what he did, including the colossal mistake that was Mao's Great Leap Forward, an attempt at agricultural reform in the period from 1958 to 1961 that ended with the death from starvation of up to 35 million people. Such was his advocacy that the creation of the 'cult' of Mao Tse-tung was sometimes credited to Lin. In many photographs I'd seen, which were later printed onto official Communist Party teacups and plates, there was Mao beside a beaming Lin Biao, who was often clutching a copy of the *Little Red Book*, the bestselling compilation of the thoughts of the illustrious leader. Lin was famous for saying, 'I don't have any talent. What I know, I learnt from Mao.' You could not have found a more weasel-like politician, but this passivity obviously appealed to Mao and, years later in 1969, as a reward for his devotion, Lin was made second-in-command of the Communist Party. What then transpired, however, is still a matter of conjecture.

Their relationship began to unwind when Lin was accused of calling Mao's then wife, Jiang Qing, a 'long-nosed pit viper', which of course she was, but you just didn't go around saying that. Mao responded by 'purging' known Lin supporters, a common tactic that often ended in the 'purged' being led away in chains to some appallingly dark and dingy cell for the rest of their natural lives. In 1971, those who remained, including Lin himself, began planning to kill Mao by sabotaging his train; at the last minute, however, Mao changed his plans and the plot was exposed.

Just over a week later, only two years after being anointed as Mao's most trusted comrade, Lin Biao came to a sticky end on 13 September, when the plane in which he was escaping to Moscow with his wife and son crashed into the frozen steppes of Mongolia. An eyewitness said the tail was on fire before it hit the ground, which led to the rumour that it had been shot down. The Party said that the word of a Mongolian herdsman was not to be trusted and that the plane had simply run out of fuel. Shortly afterwards however, over 1,000 people connected with Lin were arrested and the 'Lin Biao Incident', as the whole episode came to be known, was confined to history.

But what Mao didn't realise was that with Lin gone, so too was the voice that had for so long heartily sung his praises. Mao's mistakes and excesses through the decades were now being roundly criticised by the Communist Party faithful — and there was no one left to defend him. In this way, Mao's eventual fall from grace through the rest of the 1970s was partly his own doing.

＊＊

The guard downstairs had woken and been alerted to my presence by the two old ladies from the church. I took some photos of the rooms and went back downstairs to leave, belatedly buying a ticket as I did so. The text was all Chinese and there was no English translation, as was the case in the guidebook the guard produced from a drawer in his table — proof that this was not a place that expected to attract much foreign interest. As I turned to go, he put out his hand and gestured that I give him something; not money, he said, but the notebook I'd shown to the two ladies earlier, the one that described in Mandarin the mission I was on, which they had obviously told him about. The two women pointed to my shoulder bag and smiled. Perhaps, I mused, as I unzipped it and withdrew the book, I'd been wrong about them after all.

With his heavily veined and wrinkled hands, he fumbled with the pages until he found the one he was looking for. Slowly his eyes went back and forth, taking in each line with much concentration. Finally, after some thought, he pushed his glasses back onto the bridge of his nose and took a pen out of his drawer. Then, with some difficulty, he turned to a fresh page and began to write. For some weeks this text would stay in my notebook, almost forgotten, a spidery scrawl of black, strange-looking characters, until I could find someone who spoke English well enough to translate it for me. It turned out he'd written an old Chinese proverb that went something like this: *Near to rivers, we recognise fish; near to mountains, we recognise the songs of birds.* It took me a while to fathom these words, but in the end I realised their meaning. He was referring to my search for information on Little Mao, and telling me where best to find it. Underneath this he'd written the name of a town.

It was Yudu.

TWELVE

Taking a short cut in China is not always to be recommended. From Moxi, I thought I would be clever and take one of the back roads through Shimian to the town of Wusihe, which would then provide a fast route to Chengdu, the capital of Sichuan. Only, the woman at the bus station in Shimian said the journey onwards to Wusihe was impossible because mudslides had wiped out the road. Outside the sun shone brightly from an azure blue sky. How could there be mudslides when there was no rain, I said to her, but she was in no mood for argument and shut the ticket office door on me. Feeling bullish, I persuaded a taxi driver to take me as far along the road as possible. 'Hah,' I thought to myself, as I jumped into the front passenger seat. 'I'll show her.'

Ten kilometres on and the road had indeed turned to a muddy slush. Clouds came from nowhere and a light rain was soon falling that gradually increased to a downpour. Every so often we had to veer round large rocks that had fallen from the cliff somewhere high above us on the left, while on the right the turbulent Dadu River ran parallel to our course. We were hemmed in by fragile rocks and raging water. Still, I confidently mused, this was nothing compared to the hair-raising roads I had already endured coming down from the soaring peaks of Qinghai. So we pressed on regardless, albeit at a suitably sedate pace. It was only when the windscreen wipers packed it in that I began to reconsider the situation. It had been hard enough to see the way forward when they were working, never mind through the veil of water that poured down the glass in great, uninterrupted torrents when they stopped. The only thing to do now was to turn back.

But even that was easier said than done. Managing a U-turn on that narrow piece of roadway involved me getting out in the rain and directing the taxi driver backwards and forwards, a few centimetres at a time, until we were finally pointing in the opposite direction. Then we slowly headed back towards Shimian. But the Law of Murphy was now working overtime and bad was turning to worse. No sooner had we turned the next corner than a rockslide came into view that threatened to cut off our retreat. Rocks the size of tennis balls were still rolling down the slope, indicating that the slide had only just happened, and occasionally something larger crashed past and hit the ground then bounced over the edge to smash into the river 20 metres below. The question was, if we waited, would the slide only get worse and soon cover the road completely? The driver inched us forward. Clearly he was opting for Plan B, which was to attempt to ride over the rubble while at least two wheels could still be in contact with firm ground.

I remembered long before being in Afghanistan in the back of a captured Russian troop carrier with a group of swarthy Afghan mujahedeen, about to run the gauntlet of a stretch of dusty road that was within mortar range of a government position. In such a situation, atheists might cross their fingers or touch a lucky charm around their neck. Christians might cross themselves and repent their sins. But these men were Muslims and the murmur that went through the group that day was a prayer to Allah that we would stay safe. However, as the shells exploded behind, ahead and on either side of us, I instead put my faith in the driver of the truck, who knew exactly what he was doing as he continually altered our path, swerving closer to the fort and then away, never giving the gunners a consistent range to work with.

Now, in a similar situation but in a different country, I was about to do that again. This driver, whose name I didn't know and who naturally didn't know mine, advanced with growing speed towards the ramp of earth and rock and suddenly we were on what felt like a 40-degree angle, riding up and over the slip, the wheels spinning frantically as they sought to grip. My head hit the roof as we bounced into the air, then I was thrown to the side and back again — I remember looking down upon the Dadu River and thinking how cold and menacing it looked. With nothing to hang onto, I felt like I was in a pinball machine, getting whacked from all sides. For a brief moment we almost stopped, as the car tipped forward and the rear wheels hung uselessly in the air — the thought struck me that a puncture right now would possibly be the end of us — but then, with an almighty thud, they touched back down, the driver changed to a lower gear and, when I next opened my eyes, we were on clear, level road again.

The driver whistled through gritted teeth, then patted the steering wheel affectionately. If this man had a god, it was quite possibly the God of Motor Mechanics, whose good grace had just allowed us to pass.

A few hours later, drenched and a little bruised, but at least in one piece, we rolled back into Shimian. That was when the driver told me what had happened just a few months before. A minibus from a rival company had been lost to the same turbulent, brown waters that flowed down through the valley. Its driver had survived, but one of his two passengers, a French backpacker on holiday with her boyfriend, had not.

The next day I met the minibus driver in question. His mother ran the upstairs hostel beside the bus station where I was staying, while his brother sold cellphones from the little shop below it. The minibus driver worked for both of them, these days preferring a job behind a desk rather than a steering wheel. I asked him to tell me how the accident had happened, but he shook his head and looked away. His brother, however, was more forthcoming. He told a story of a rainy morning with the river at its peak, filled with the snowmelt of early spring, and how the tourists had paid double to get to Wusihe — they had a connecting flight home from Chengdu to catch and were desperate not to miss it. But somewhere along the way, while the minibus was squeezing past a truck going in the opposite direction, the road had given way under its wheels, plunging it into the torrent and filling it with water instantly. The driver and the Frenchman had been swept out through the shattered remains of the front windscreen and barely made it to the riverbank. But within seconds the current had spun the bus around 180 degrees and the full force of the river had then poured through the minibus, pinning the Frenchwoman to the rear seat.

'Very sad,' said the brother. 'She was a nice girl.'

Because there were no other roads I had to backtrack all the way to Kangding, a haul of over 20 hours on some of the most rutted tracks conceivable. The other passengers were Yao peasant women in black hats and funereal dresses. However, the road from Kangding eventually joined an expressway and, for the first time in what seemed like ages, the journey was thereafter swift and smooth.

Chengdu appeared as night fell, the first large city I'd seen since Shanghai, and within an hour the driver had dropped us all off at a nondescript point on the edge of its almighty urban sprawl. It wasn't ideal. While the other passengers were climbing into waiting cars and speeding off to their homes, I had to work out what to do next. Fortunately, a taxicab appeared, and after some negotiation, we agreed on a price to get me to the city centre and, I hoped, a bed for the night.

The glow of electric lights bounced off the low clouds that were beginning to gather over the city. A light rain was falling and the driver flicked a switch to activate his windscreen wipers, but nothing happened. He thumped the dashboard, which persuaded them to swish back and forth a few times before they halted mid-windscreen, as if pausing for breath, unsure whether to carry on or go back. I felt like that myself. Unsure what to do next, and with only a small slip of paper bearing the name of a university professor in Changsha to go on, I began to sense the enormity of my task. For a start, Changsha was still 1,200 kilometres away.

That being said, my journey was somewhat easier than the one He Zizhen had encountered. Having left Yudu, the long marchers endeavoured to escape Chiang Kai-shek's superior forces by avoiding Sichuan and heading south then west into the provinces of Guizhou and Yunnan. Along the way, in February 1935, He Zizhen gave birth to a baby daughter, who was immediately left with a local family, along with a small amount of money and a few bowls of opium as payment. He Zizhen hardly got a look at the child and never had time to give her a name, such was the marchers' haste. Then, two months later, a bomb dropped from a reconnaissance aircraft left her with terrible shrapnel injuries to her back and head. She almost died, but somehow pulled through even though the following weeks of her convalescence happened not in the comfort and care of a hospital bed, but on a rough stretcher carried by porters. Mao would not agree to leaving her behind for treatment, and insisted she went with him.

In comparison I had nothing to complain about, but I couldn't shake the overall feeling of tiredness that began to hinder me. I had been on the road for what seemed like forever, covering enormous distances, often at a snail's pace. But I knew the problem was more than just physical. A growing sense of doubt was seeping into my consciousness. I needed more than a good night's sleep, which at least I was sure would come at this lower elevation. I needed something far more primitive, far more basic, something that is essential on any journey. More than ever, I required a gentle touch from the hand of Lady Luck.

* * *

In Moxi, the hills go on and on

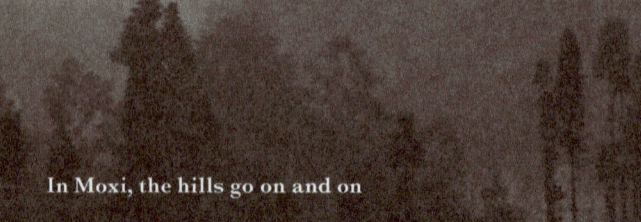

In central Chengdu, the Gateway Inn provided all the necessities of life: a warm bed and a window — from which I could see the top of Mao's head in the morning. The mighty statue of him, built in 1969 to a height of 12.26 metres, to match the date of his birthday, had captured my imagination the last time I had wandered through this city almost two decades before. Then, his shadow had fallen over a multitude of cyclists who crowded the roadway to such a degree that if they had stayed still you could have walked across the road on their tightly compacted shoulders. Now the stone giant looked down upon a teeming traffic system where the car ruled and the cyclist was shunted to the side. Exactly what Mao would have felt about this could not be known, though Mao was no enemy of progress — at the height of patriotic fervour during his reign, for example, many of Chengdu's oldest and most beautiful buildings were torn down to make way for the 'new China'. Nevertheless, I wondered what he would have thought about the fact that the younger generation of students preferred a computer screen to a book or lecture theatre.

I came across a backstreet Internet café filled with students on chat lines with their friends, playing games and smoking Hongtashan cigarettes, the most popular and cheapest brand in China. Fortunately for me, I was the perfect, alternative form of entertainment. Polite, eager faces pressed towards me with their heavily accented versions of 'Hello!' and 'How are you?' A seat at a vacant screen was found and a crowd gathered to watch my clumsy attempts at negotiating a Chinese keyboard. Helpful advice eventually steered me to an English version of the homepage I wanted, a Chinese search engine that would reveal more about Changsha University. In the end I needn't have bothered. Once I'd started typing, the subject of my search brought an immediate outpouring of information. Apparently there was quite a number of students at Chengdu University who were from Changsha.

'Excuse me,' said one young voice. 'I am Hong.'

I turned to face a slim, afro-haired boy who was trying his best to grow a wispy moustache. 'Why are you interested in Changsha University? It is very small and not very interesting. Chengdu is much better.'

The boy wore purple flared trousers and a gold silk shirt, and hid behind a pair of large dark glasses. If he was trying to look like an Oriental version of a '70s rock star he was doing a very good job. I told him I was looking for a professor who taught there, but the name on the piece of paper didn't ring any bells. Very soon, however, the precise nature of my search had reached even the furthest corners of the room and more than a few interesting leads. One of these was particularly exciting. Chengdu University naturally had its own experts on Chinese history, but it just so happened there was also a foreign researcher who was attached to the department, an American no less. Would I like to meet him asked the boy in flared trousers?

'Is the Pope Catholic?' I replied.

He looked at me quizzically, head tilted to one side.

'Very much so,' I added quickly, and he beamed with delight.

'English expressions,' he shrugged. 'There are so many.'

He went to make a few phone calls and returned a short while later with a broad grin on his face. He had traced the name and number of the American and said I could ring him the next morning and organise a meeting — which meant, he then pointed out, that I was free go out with him and his friends.

'You like dancing?' he asked.

Judging by what he was wearing, it was unlikely that Hong was going to be a huge fan of classical ballet or Irish folk dancing. Sure enough, the treat he had in store for me was a long way from anything middle-of-the-road. Soon we were walking down steps into a completely different world. The club was his older brother's and operated from an underground cellar a block from the Internet café. A neon sign above the door was the only indicator of its existence and we were let in only when someone on the other side of the door had checked us out via a security camera. The door opened automatically, with a resounding click, and we found ourselves in a long corridor with a concrete floor and walls that seemed to stretch ahead forever. Soon, however, the unmistakable thump of dance music came closer and closer, and we rounded a corner and walked up to another heavy security door that was opened for us by an unseen hand. Without missing a step, we were in — and what a place it turned out to be.

Strobe lighting illuminated in brief flashes a wide dance floor on which a crowd of Chengdu's hip, cool things were going for it. At the rear was a bar where, while my eyes and ears adjusted, my host went and bought some beer. His friends were already grooving to a hypnotic dance track that sounded like German Techno on acid. It was fast and furious, 150 beats per minute, and the dancers' arms and bodies were a flurry of rhythmic shapes in the dim light. It was amazing, but the wall of sound was intense and I had to retreat as far as possible from the monstrous speaker systems that dominated the back wall. Fortunately, that took me to the bar, where I found Hong. He was shouting into the ear of the bartender and gesturing in my direction. Seconds later we were clinking bottles of beer and trying to have a conversation. This would have been hard enough in a nightclub in my own country, but in China it proved to be nigh-on impossible.

Eventually Hong gave up and took me by the arm to a chill-out lounge area behind the bar. It was a blessed respite, perhaps also because the air was suddenly permeated with the smell of marijuana. I was getting high just by breathing, and it wasn't the only drug doing the rounds. A young girl was snorting coke from her girlfriend's bare shoulder, before they both floated past me in a fit of giggles. Meanwhile Hong was knocking back shots of tequila and motioned for me to do the same. I had a couple before Cocaine Girl reappeared and, before I knew it, I was being led to the dance floor to try and keep up with the frenetic pace of the music. It was impossible, so I decided the best thing to do was just stand there and let it wash over me, wave upon wave of noise that threatened to turn my brain into mush. Maybe this looked cool (although somehow I doubted it), because quite soon after I was joined by others who also stood stock-still in a zombie-like trance. Perhaps I had just given rise to a new dance, even though it was born more out of pain than inspiration. If so, that was going to be my last contribution for the night. It might have been an hour, but most likely it was a lot less, before I called time on the whole underworld dance adventure. The quiet of the concrete corridor was a welcome relief as I made good my escape, unnoticed by Hong or his friends, and returned the way we had come. It might have been impolite, but the ringing in my ears told me I had no alternative.

* * *

The American researcher turned out to be a 28-year-old from Utah; he was called Dale but had a Polish family name.

'Wozniacki,' he said, 'but back home they call me Woz.'

How an American with Polish parents came to be in one of the biggest universities in China teaching English and history was soon explained. He'd attended Vancouver's University of British Columbia, majoring in Political Science, and had lived in a district called Yaletown. Somehow, in China, this had resulted in the not-so-insignificant misunderstanding that Dale was actually a distinguished graduate of Yale, the Ivy League university. I laughed, which made him flinch.

'Yeah I know,' he said somewhat sheepishly. 'It's kinda embarrassing. But I don't want to disappoint these kids. They want to think I'm from Yale Uni, so let 'em. You hungry, by the way? Want to get some noodles?'

We'd met at the entrance to the university, which wasn't far from a typical open-air food stall. We sat on cane stools at a low wooden table and he ordered for both of us in fluent Mandarin.

'Hope you like hot food,' he asked. 'Sichuan dishes will blow your head off if you're not careful, but this place is okay.'

While we waited, I explained what, or to be more precise, who I was looking for and he had a number of interesting, if not very pragmatic, ideas. The first was that I simply go to the last place the boy had been seen and look there. I replied that I was just as interested in how people felt about Mao An Hong and his infamous dad, and that the journey en route to that region gave me the opportunity to find out. Having said that, I told him, not many people I'd met so far had been very forthcoming on the topic. I'd had a lot of polite smiles and nods of the head, but not a great deal of significant revelations.

'Okay,' he said. 'Maybe I can help.'

He gestured to the woman running the restaurant and she came over. Dale pointed at me and spoke to her fluently. She listened intently as she dried her hands on her apron. Occasionally her eyes would dart from him to me, looking me up and down. When he'd finished she was joined by an elderly man with grey hair poking out from under his hat, who'd been listening in on the conversation. The two of them exchanged a few words in such a strong local dialect that even Dale had trouble understanding. Eventually, however, we discovered that the old man had been a Red Guard in his youth and that he had been stationed in Jiangxi province for many years, not far from a place called Jinggangshan. He smiled when I recognised the name of the town and puffed out his chest proudly. Jinggangshan was well known as the birthplace of the Chinese Revolution; the Red Army had hidden from the Nationalists in the surrounding mountains. Mao himself had spent a lot of time there, plotting and scheming to bring down the government. Apparently, at one of the hideouts there was a 700-year-old tree that Mao regularly sat under, sketching out his tactics in the soil between its giant roots. People said the power of this great tree worked through Mao, proving that nature was on the side of the Communists.

When the old man had finished waxing lyrical about the Glorious Revolution, I got Dale to ask if he knew anything of the boy, Little Mao, but again came the same response — a shrug of the shoulders and a shake of the head. It was as if I was chasing something that was of no importance to anyone but me. Surely, I said to Dale, someone must regard a missing child, particularly one fathered by the supreme leader of the Communist Party, as worthy of investigation. He could sense my growing frustration, so he said he would check in the university data banks to see if anything popped up.

'But don't get your hopes up,' he added, sliding a steaming bowl of noodle soup across the table. 'One thing I do know about the Chinese. When it comes to the history of their Communist Revolution, if what you're looking for doesn't fit with the official version of events, and I'm thinking this kid does not, it gets removed from the records pretty quickly. You may as well be searching for a ghost.'

I stabbed my chopsticks into the noodles and stirred them round to let the steam rise like a vaporous apparition.

'Maybe,' I said finally, blowing on a mouthful. 'But even ghosts deserve to have their stories told.'

* * *

Dale's office was a small cupboard of a room next to an actual cupboard that contained the mops the cleaners used on the floors each night. He squeezed in behind his desk and turned on his computer. I noticed a calendar on the wall that his mother had sent him, with pictures of snowy mountains and spring flowers in Vancouver. He said she was Canadian but had married an American academic and they had ended up in Utah, near Salt Lake City.

'Dad's a Mormon, Mum is Catholic,' he said, shaking his head. 'It's not an easy mix.'

I asked him if that was why he went to university in Canada and he replied, somewhat sadly, 'Pretty much. Anywhere, just so long as it wasn't around the old man. It didn't help that I'm agnostic.'

Dale started searching through the files and uncovered little of interest. Hunched over the screen, he was going through them saying, 'Nah', 'Nope', 'Nada', 'Zip' until, at the bottom of one page, he stopped. There was a brief mention of a Chinese journalist, from a small local paper in the town of Ganzhou in Jiangxi province, who had had a similar interest to mine. I moved round to Dale's side and peered at the screen. It was in Chinese but there was a colour photo of a slightly worried looking man, about 30 years old, in a white shirt and, next to him, the shoulder of a taller man in a darker, short-sleeved shirt. The photo had been tightly cropped, cutting out the rest of the taller man.

'This is interesting,' said Dale, speaking the words slowly as he ran a finger along a line of type. 'It says the guy in the white shirt is a journalist who was also looking for Little Mao, with some success apparently.'

'Is that it?'

'Almost,' said Dale. 'It also says there was no evidence to support his theory, so the story had not been taken seriously.'

'And this was when?'

Dale scrolled to the top and found the date of the article. It was only a few years old.

'And something tells me,' said Dale, scrolling back down, 'that the shoulder in this photo belongs to the person he had found, although someone clearly hasn't wanted that person in the picture.'

'You think it's Mao's son?' I asked.

Dale thought for a few seconds and then said, 'Well, look at this journalist's face. He looks like he's quite nervous and anxious, but in a respectful kind of way. As if he's standing next to an important official.'

'Like someone older?'

'Yeah, definitely,' he said. 'Respect for your elders is very important to the Chinese, and there's no question this guy is acting very respectfully.'

It also seemed the article had been edited, with the last paragraph ending prematurely in a way that suggested there might have been more written on the subject, so that was all Dale could glean from it.

I had been given another clue, a place called Ganzhou, but little else. Still, even that was an enormous step forward. I was excited, more than ever before. The fact that someone else had been along this path was thrilling, because it meant there was an actual path. Part of my problem was that it sometimes felt as if I was on a wild goose chase, running after shadows and nothing more. Here at least was proof of something solid and tangible.

Dale stood up and found an atlas of China on his shelf. He flicked open the cover and thumbed through the pages until he came to Jiangxi province, then followed the main road south from Nanchang to Yongxin, then onto a series of much smaller rural roads through Jinggangshan to Ganzhou, which was underlined on the map, signifying a largish town rather than a village. Even more exciting were the two names just above it and to the right: Yudu and Ruijin. These were places of great importance to me because, according to all the history books, it was in this area that Mao had begun the Long March. Pursued by the advancing forces of Chiang Kai-shek, he and his poor, long-suffering wife He Zizhen had departed in great haste. And it was somewhere near these locations that they had left behind their two-year-old son, Little Mao, whom they would never see again.

A man sports a straw helmet in Chengdu

In Chengdu, commuters pay little attention to Mao

THIRTEEN

THE NIGHT TRAIN TO CHANGSHA WASN'T THE EXPRESS KIND: IT WAS slow to leave and slow to arrive. Even when it did lurch forward from the station in a way that suggested the beginning of our journey, it stopped moments later and waited, without any clear reason, for another hour or more. What made it worse was the heat. And in Changsha the temperature was likely to be even hotter — it was one of the four 'furnace cities' of Central China. 'Patience is a virtue', I reminded myself, echoing the advice of the German-speaking monk on the steps of Kumbum Monastery near Xining.

My ordeal made me wonder what must have been going through the mind of He Zizhen as she had followed dutifully in the steps of her husband during those first, long, hard months of the march. Did she still believe she would be reunited one day with her son? Was it 'patience' she displayed back then, a hopeful optimism, or the grim determination of a soldier, and a mother, to make that happen? Something told me it was closer to the second of these two. I'd read enough to know this woman would not go quietly, allowing fate to take over. She was a fighter, a revolutionary and the intellectual equal of the greatest leader China had ever known. She would not give up, not while she was still breathing.

As time went on, I thought less and less about Mao and more about He Zizhen. In my mind I had begun to see her as the real hero of the march, and therefore perhaps the real story to be explored. What she endured, both physically and mentally, outweighed possibly anything her male counterparts might have experienced. Over the course of the march she was shot at by Nationalist soldiers, strafed by their warplanes, even bombed — in fact the injuries she would suffer from that explosion would hinder her for the rest of her days. No one could say she had shirked from her duties or run from danger, although sometimes I wondered whether as much could be said of her husband.

The three men I shared the hard-sleeper compartment with were squatting in the aisle and eyeing everyone intently. They wore blue trousers rolled up to their knees, revealing calf muscles that were sharp and clearly defined, shaped by years of hard work. The dust on their shoes and jackets set them apart from the other worker-commuters who were heading home for the weekend, men with stomachs that bulged out over their trouser belts, who carried leather attaché cases like badges of rank and regiment. The three squatters looked ill-at-ease in this company and the businessmen equally unhappy with the workers' untidy presence. One man in a shiny grey suit took it upon himself to berate the guard and demand these men make an immediate exit, not only for everyone's safety but also for the wellbeing of the 'foreigner'. I looked down the aisle, saw no one else who fitted this description, and realised he was talking about me. It turned out though that, because it was full, the three men had received an 'upgrade' from the uncomfortable but dirt-cheap seat-only section in the next-door carriage. So the guard ignored the man's requests to have them removed and let the trio stay for the night. As the guard walked past collecting tickets, he stopped and, with great ceremony, clicked my ticket with a practised air of officialdom, then threw a mocking glance back at the business elite.

The man with the shiny suit warned me to sleep lightly and guard my things against any thieving fingers. He was in the insecticide business, he said, and presented me with a business card that was embossed with gold writing. It read 'Michael Wu, Managing Director of Hubei Industries' and then, in brackets, 'Poisons Division'.

'Before 1979,' said Mr Wu, 'farmers used natural pesticides and their crops were often wiped out by plagues of insects. Now they use my chemical products.'

'Are they safe?' I asked.

'One hundred per cent safe and one hundred per cent effective,' he replied, not without a certain professional pride. 'Very powerful chemicals at a very low price.'

China had major environmental problems thanks to chemicals like these. They leached into the soil, entering the water table and therefore drinking water. Hubei province was one of the worst affected regions, and its air was heavily polluted too. Pesticides had been found in the snow on Tibet's highest peaks, carried there by strong winds from land many thousands of kilometres away. Eco-friendly products were available, but they were 10 times the price of Mr Wu's low-cost synthetic options, so farmers had little choice. It's a common scenario around the world of course, especially in the developing world, where agricultural communities strive to feed their ever-increasing domestic populations through higher yields. But China's problem is that the use of pesticides is uncontrolled and this has resulted in large areas of arable land becoming infertile. The Chinese government's 'solution' is to use the trillion or so of export-related US dollars it has managed to 'hoover' up like a giant vacuum cleaner over the years to buy up huge tracts of land in places like Australia and America for growing food for their future generations. Even clean and green New Zealand has been earmarked as China's dairy farm.

'This is all for the good of the people,' said a benevolent Mr Wu. But when he looked around the carriage, his eyes fell upon the three dusty workers camped in the corridor and his compassion faded to a scowl.

It turned out he had good reason to be unhappy, though. At Changsha the next morning, the three men were gone and so was Mr Wu's leather attaché case. His anger was apocalyptic and, the last I saw of him, he was speeding past the window on the platform outside, looking for the police, his face puce with rage.

I jumped down from the carriage and made my own, more sedate way into town. The taxi driver dropped me at his brother's hotel and I paid for a night in advance. The manager asked if I wanted to pay 'extra' for a massage, then gestured towards the three pretty girls in short skirts who were lounging on a sofa. Next to them was a table with an old style telephone on top of a pile of magazines. Politely, I declined the massage, but asked if I could use his phone instead. He agreed, probably thinking this was a strange choice, and waved at the girls to make some space so that I could sit down. With their help I managed to contact the university, asking for the professor whose name I had been given back in Garze. But the university hadn't heard of him. It seemed as if I had encountered yet another dead end.

One of the girls introduced herself as Ning, part-time masseuse, mum and librarian. It was Ning's job to sort out returned books at the Hunan Library, a job that probably paid less than pummelling the tired limbs of hotel guests, but one which was far more pleasant.

'The air conditioning is very good. In summer when Changsha becomes an oven, the library is lovely and cool.'

Ning took me there later that day and showed me to an English section where I was able to read a book on the history of the city. As well as being relentlessly attacked by the Japanese in the late 1930s and early 1940s, and for a brief period captured by them before being retaken by Chiang Kai-shek in 1944, it was also the city in which Mao's second wife lost her life. In 1930, Yang Kahui lived on the outskirts of Changsha in relative peace and quiet, until Mao laid siege to the city with his army of Communists and the local Nationalist commander ordered her to be tried and killed. Had Mao thought to protect her in some way before he attacked? Reading between the lines, even in this pro-Mao history book, it seemed that was not the case. Though he wrote about his grief later, in letters and poems, it could not disguise the fact that he simply did not care for anyone other than himself.

I visited Yang Kahui's home and found it had been turned into a kind of shrine to touristy knicknacks and Party propaganda.

Souvenir sellers displayed their wares, which bizarrely included soft-porn paperbacks and a giant jade phallus. Leafing through the books I found myself talking to a young man who said he was a hydro engineer, overnighting in Changsha on his way home to Beijing. I asked him if building dams was a good career and he agreed, but added that it was dangerous. There had been 12 recent fatalities in Sichuan's hydro industry alone, he said, before returning to his salacious and well-thumbed novel.

I wandered off, but before I left he came up to me, almost apologetically, and tapped me on the shoulder.

'You know, China is built on such tragedies,' he said.

* * *

The next day I wasted little time and took the morning train straight to Nanchang, then in the afternoon located the bus station that serviced all of the roads heading south. Nanchang was a famous city in Communist Party circles. People called it the 'City of Heroes' after the men and women here who became the first Communists to take up arms against the Nationalist government, during an uprising in 1927. But my main interest lay elsewhere. There was a bus leaving that day for Jinggangshan and I was soon travelling with a host of Chinese families with young school-age children, who were eager to see another famous home of the Communist Revolution. There was much excitement, chiefly because of the adventurous journey they were undertaking, but also because I was making it with them. One young boy was already dressed up in a light blue military suit and peaked cap adorned with fake gold braid and a red star at its centre. From the seat opposite he smiled then snapped his heels together and saluted.

Outside the windows, rural China rolled past in neatly squared off sections of arable farmland. Every square centimetre was planted and tended; even some rooftops sprouted cabbages and pumpkins. Here, droughts were rare and water aplenty washed down the gutters and channels to nourish the farmers' fields. Tall crops of barley waved from the roadside and, beyond these, yellow-flowering rapeseed burst forth in a riot of colour. All of this under a bright blue sky bordered with lush green mountains in the distance.

These were the same plains the soldiers of Chiang Kai-shek had marched over in the late 1920s and early '30s, aiming for the same far-off Jinggang Mountains, where not only thieves and robbers lurked, but a good number of the earliest Communist supporters. There were deep valleys nestled in those ranges that you could hide in for years, and indeed Mao had united his armies from Jiangxi province there, along with those from the neighbouring Hunan region, for that very reason. Having brokered peace with the thugs and criminals in hiding there, who no doubt shared an equal hatred for all government forces, he was free to come and go as he pleased for the most part, choosing when and where to confront his enemy. But when that enemy became too strong, not even the deepest mountain fortress was safe.

I had a romantic notion of Jinggangshan as a tiny, quaint, history-laden village, but the reality was far removed from this. Although small, pretty and tree-lined, Jinggangshan had been turned into a tourist mecca for Red Travellers bent on spending their holidays revelling in former revolutionary glories. It was clean swept and immaculately presented, but this fuelled my doubt that it had either heart or soul. Tourism can be like a surgeon's scalpel at times, removing the character of a place and leaving an ugly scar behind.

It was just on evening and the central square was crowded with the young and old, talking and chatting, drinking tea and eating ice cream. It was warm and muggy, without a breath of wind to disturb the lights that hung from the camphor trees. Kenny Rogers crooned a love song from a number of loudspeakers mounted on wooden poles, while children in clean white shirts and pretty dresses played tag beneath them. A man who owned a nearby hotel struck up a conversation as I watched all this from a bench. He started off trying to sell me a room — a very special room. Visiting dignitaries used it when they came to Jinggangshan, even the state governor of Jiangxi, he said. It came with a large bed, a view of the mountains and a pretty young girl who would attend to my every wish. I said I already had a room and he asked where, so I pointed across the road to the hotel I had chosen. It was quite expensive, but there was nothing cheaper in the village that I could find. He scrunched up his nose in horror and warned me that the bed would be small, there would be a view of the alley and the girl would be ugly.

I left him and walked into the middle of the square. Small children scattered or clung to their mothers' skirts as I passed. Just at that moment, the crowd of people around me started to organise themselves into straight lines and, as I watched, Kenny Rogers was replaced with something even more unexpected: line dancing.

I was in the middle of a good old-fashioned Chinese hoedown. There were no cowboy hats or boots and jeans, just little old men and middle-aged women in loose-fitting trousers that looked like they doubled as pyjama bottoms, gyrating their hips and shuffling their feet in perfect formation to Dwight Yoakam's 'Crazy Little Thing Called Love'. The young generally stood back and looked on as their parents and grandparents performed their synchronised moves, but not in embarrassment; it was more like respect. One female line dancer saw that I was watching and immediately started putting on a show, standing straighter and adopting a stern expression of concentration, as if this were a competition. Unfortunately, the gentleman to her right was not quite as competent and she became flustered by his ill-timed steps and eventually sought out the company of better dancers a few rows on.

It was, without a doubt, one of my most bizarre experiences in China. Here was one of the world's oldest civilisations, which, over several thousand years, had given us such things as paper, gunpowder and the compass. And what had we given it in return? Line dancing. I wondered what we would give them next: *Saturday Night Fever*, *Grease* perhaps, or maybe ballroom. In which case, if it took off in this massive country of over 1.3 billion, it might completely exhaust the world's supply of sequins.

Still chuckling, I wandered off to my humble room with no view and no personal services, to sleep and dream of a Chinese Elvis, in a white silk suit with a red star on the back, who takes over the world and forces everyone to sing 'Jailhouse Rock' while following him on a long walk to nowhere.

Graffiti on bamboo near
Jinggangshan: 'Peng was here'

FOURTEEN

The Luoxian Mountains around Jinggangshan were cloaked in a mist that happily made it several degrees cooler on the slopes than down in the village. I had woken early and been persuaded to get onto the pillion seat of a small motorbike by a young local soldier who called himself Joe. He was about 24, of average height but with the physique of someone who looked like he knew his way round a judo ring. He was dressed in the standard green army uniform but wore socks and sandals on his feet instead of boots. As we climbed higher and higher, Joe sang revolutionary songs and excitedly pointed out places of historical interest.

'There is the tree our great and illustrious Communist Leader Mao Tse-tung climbed in order to speak to his victorious troops. And, over there, that is the rock our great and illustrious Communist Leader Mao Tse-tung sat upon and devised tactics for his victorious troops.'

By the time Joe had finished describing whatever event had taken place we were usually well past the actual site. It didn't matter though. Colourful they might have been, but somehow I doubted the veracity of his stories and put them down to exuberance rather than a sound grasp of history. My suspicions were further aroused when Joe described the mist that surrounded us and wet our hair as we zoomed along. He said it was the same mist that 'our great and illustrious Communist Leader Mao Tse-tung used to conceal his victorious troops'.

'The same mist?' I queried.

'Yes,' Joe replied. 'The same mist exactly.'

Then he burst forth with the first lines of another operatic song while waving one hand as if he were conducting an orchestra.

It took half an hour to reach the top of Jinggang Mountain, where Joe said we would find the remains of one of Mao's hideouts. As we pulled over to the side of the road, the sun broke through the cloud and began to dry us out. From this vantage point I could look out over the forests, following the jungle-clad mountainsides as they sloped down to the plains below. Ridge after ridge stretched into the distance, with the furthest one barely discernible against the grey-green misty horizon.

Just as hazy was the precise location of Mao's hideout. A tourist guide, who'd just arrived by coach with her group of gawking Chinese tourists, directed them amongst some shallow ditches that looked like they'd been recently dug out with pickaxes. They were deep enough to squat in and their position was a commanding one, overlooking the valley, but it was hardly an impressive historical site.

As always, however, Joe was enthusiastic. He peered down into the trenches as one would into the recently unveiled tomb of Tutankhamun. Each clod of earth was a sacred relic. He even tsk-tsked at a red-scarved Chinese woman who had the gall to jump down into one of the ditches and pose for a photo. Apologetically, she climbed out, but, as far as Joe was concerned, the damage was done.

'Beijing tourists,' he whispered contemptuously. 'Who do they think they are?'

Not all that Joe had to say on his country's history was complete hyperbole, however. There were some things that rang true that could be backed up by recognised sources, notably records compiled by several foreign observers who maintained an interest in the early development of Communism during the 1920s and '30s. One of these was the American journalist Edgar Snow, famous for his 1937 book *Red Star Over China*, an account of his dealings with Mao and other party leaders of the time. In the book, Snow details the way the Communists adopted a policy of 'non-confrontation' with government troops, fearing they could be wiped out by the enemy's superior forces if they met them in a pitched battle. Joe reminded me of this when he waved an arm over the forested land below us and commented that it was dense enough to hide a hundred thousand men.

'Behind every tree was a brave Red Army soldier,' he said.

Instead of tackling Chiang Kai-shek's armies head on, the Communists of Jinggangshan used guerrilla tactics, staging sudden attacks on key strategic posts or supply lines and then, as quickly as they had come, disappearing from view. These attacks were highly successful in slowing down the advance of government forces as well as destroying their morale. Sometimes the Reds would come away with more than captured guns and ammunition too. Government troops regularly defected to the Communists, joining what they saw as the 'People's Army' as opposed to a government one. After all, the Communists could boast an ideology that sought to remove power from the landowners and hand it back to the peasant class, and the peasant classes made up a significant proportion of Chiang Kai-shek's army. Land was like gold, and the lure of ownership was an extremely attractive proposition to any man or woman.

Eventually the success of the Red Army attacks forced Chiang Kai-shek to change tack, and in the early 1930s he began to encircle the Communists with a network of thousands of 'turtle-shell' forts and well-entrenched artillery lines with overlapping fields of fire in an attempt to cut them off economically. This tactic was recommended by one of Chiang's advisors, the noted German military expert General Hans von Seeckt, who wanted to flush out the Communists from their hideouts and force them into the open. It was called the Fifth Campaign and initially it worked well. By their own accounts, the Red Army suffered 60,000 casualties during this one siege, forcing them finally to give up the offensive, leave their mountains and beat a hasty retreat. And thus the Long March was born.

Snow described how it began:

> Nevertheless, the Fifth Campaign ultimately proved inconclusive. It failed in its objective, which was to destroy the living forces of the Red Army. A Red military conference was called at Juichin, and it was decided to withdraw, transferring the main Red strength to a new base. The plans for this great expedition, which was to last a whole year, were complete and efficient.

They perhaps revealed a certain military genius that the Reds had not shown during their periods of offensive. For it is one thing to command a victorious advancing army, and quite another to carry through to success a plan calling for retreat under such handicaps as those which lay ahead in the now famous Long March to the North-west.

The retreat from Jiangxi evidently was so swiftly and secretly managed that the main forces of the Red troops, estimated at about 100,000 men, had already been marching for several days before the enemy headquarters became aware of what was taking place. They had mobilised in Southern Jiangxi, withdrawing most of their regular troops from the northern front, and replacing them with partisans. Those movements occurred always at night. When practically the whole Red Army was concentrated in Yudu, in southern Jiangxi, the order was given for the Great March, which began on October 16, 1934.

For three nights the Reds pressed in two columns to the west and to the south. On the fourth they advanced, totally unexpectedly, almost simultaneously attacking the Hunan and Kwangtung lines of fortifications. They took these by assault, put their astonished enemy on the run, and never stopped until they had occupied the ribbon of blockading forts and entrenchments on the southern front. This gave them roads to the south and to the west, along which their vanguard began its sensational trek.

Snow himself was there to witness the long lines of soldiers and peasants who carried everything away with them. Whole factories were taken apart and the machinery shouldered by people and pack animals for as many kilometres as possible, until eventually fatigue got the better of them and equipment was buried along the trail, including machine guns, ammunition and silver. Even today people sometimes dig up old rusted rifles and other relics of the past, not to mention the bones of those who didn't make it. In 1974, reports surfaced that the mummified remains of two climbers found on a glacier could be connected with the Long March — what was left of their clothes was said to closely resemble those of Red Army soldiers. But before an official excavation could take place a snowstorm covered the remains and their exact location was lost.

I mentioned this to Joe and he was genuinely upset.

'Imagine the cold,' he muttered, looking down at his sandals. 'And they had only cloth wrapped round their feet for shoes.'

In silence we rode back down the mountain to Jinggangshan and I paid him the few yuan he was asking, plus a bonus for taking me to the holy spring where Mao had once bathed. Later he introduced me to his older brother, Chang, who offered to sell me a replica Mao suit for a princely sum. I declined, telling them that my bag was not big enough to carry such things with due respect. They nodded in agreement and gave me a Mao badge instead.

'It will bring you good luck,' said Joe.

Oddly enough, he was right. That night I invited Joe and Chang to dinner at a local yum cha restaurant in Jinggangshan, just off the main square where I had watched the line dancing the night before. I insisted they would be my guests and, though it took some persuading, they eventually agreed. We ate steamed pork buns and dim sum washed down with green tea, until our stomachs bulged. During the course of the meal Chang, who was a little less excitable than his younger sibling, mentioned a period of time spent in the military and my ears pricked up. Like their grandfather and father before them, they had joined the army at an early age, but whereas Joe was in the infantry, Chang found himself in military intelligence, specialising in radar. This helped explain why his English was particularly good. He had studied at the Luoyang Foreign Language Institute, a top academy for the military's brightest stars. It was the lure of cold, hard cash that had led to him selling Mao memorabilia to Chinese tourists: the military wasn't a way to get rich and, so, given the option, he'd chosen civilian life.

'Our grandfather was stationed near here in the 1930s,' Chang said. 'His regiment fought to control the local Jiangxi warlords.'

Sensing there was more of a story here, I dug a little deeper and discovered it wasn't just the warmongering indigenous tribes of Jiangxi that his grandfather had sought to keep in check. Suddenly Joe was a little quiet, as his brother explained how the regiment had also been instructed to force the Long Marchers into the mountains and let the freezing cold do their job for them.

'So your grandfather was with Chiang Kai-shek?' I asked.

Chang nodded and Joe moved uncomfortably in his seat. It was typical of the awful conflicts that occur during civil wars, when even families can be at odds with each other and then struggle to deal with the enmity that remains. Although in Chang's case he had no such problem; it was only Joe who was in denial. Chang depicted his grandfather's military career as noble, while Joe was embarrassed by it.

'He sounds like a great man,' I said after a while, trying to ease the tension. 'What happened to him?'

Chang picked out a dim sum expertly with his chopsticks, popped the morsel into his mouth and motioned for Joe to answer. When his brother ignored him, Chang swallowed hard and said:

'Went to Taiwan.'

In 1949 when the Communists finally defeated Chiang Kai-shek, the General escaped with his two-million-strong army, plus many national treasures and a prodigious amount of gold, across the water to Taiwan and formed the Republic of China, which, to this day, is still not recognised by mainland China and, according to all reports, never will be. The Communist Party simply looks upon Taiwan as a province awaiting repatriation, either peacefully or militarily.

Fascinated by how the brothers seemed to sit at either end of the political table on this subject, but hoping to help maintain the peace, I asked Joe if he thought Chairman Mao had forgiven those soldiers who fought for the Nationalists.

'Our great and illustrious leader was famous for his big heart,' he replied, tugging at his shirt for good measure.

'So he would greet your grandfather in the same way as he would you?'

Joe lifted his head and looked around the restaurant at the dozen or so tables where Jinggangshan families were gathered.

It was as though he were imagining the Great Helmsman striding through the door at that moment, arms wide open to embrace his loyal soldier.

'Yes, I'm sure he would,' he reasoned.

'No doubt he would read some poetry too,' I ventured.

'He was a great poet,' said Joe thoughtfully.

There was a moment's pause, and then, without introduction, he got to his feet and recited one of his favourite Mao poems. When he was finished everyone in the restaurant applauded and Joe's cheeks were flushed with patriotic pride — the same rich red colour as his national flag. Chang provided the English translation. He said the poem was called 'Jinggang Mountain', and it celebrated a famous battle Mao had fought against the Nationalists, apparently not far from where Joe and I had stood that day.

Below the hills fly flags and banners,
Above the hilltops sound bugles and drums.
The foe encircles us thousands strong,
Steadfastly we stand our ground.

Already our defence is iron clad,
Now our will unites us like a fortress.
From Huangyanggai roars the thunder of cannon,
Word comes the enemy has run away in the night.

When he was finished I applauded too and, for a brief moment, in my mind's eye, glimpsed the ghostly spectre of Mao's tall figure in a light grey suit, buttoned up to the neck, with his signature black locks slicked back from a receding hairline, smiling imperiously as he stood by the door to the restaurant.

'You liked it?' asked Joe.

'I did,' I said.

My apparition was still there, waiting by the entrance to a typical yum cha restaurant in a far-flung corner of a massive country still largely devoted to his memory. Poet-philosopher, warrior chief, consummate schemer, dreamer, the Great Helmsman — all these descriptions were true. The only department in which he didn't measure up, it seemed, and for which few held him accountable, was as a father. In that sense Mao had been an abject failure.

I heard the door to the restaurant slam angrily and, when I looked in that direction again, Mao's ghost was gone.

Card players at a café, Ruijin

FIFTEEN

I WOKE BEFORE FIRST LIGHT AND STOLE A MARCH ON THE DAY, getting a few hours of walking in before a slow dawn chased away the night. I could have waited a few days for a bus to take me south, but it felt better to hit the road on foot, even though it was still dark and the distance to the villages of Ruijin and Yudu, the twin cradles of Communism, was still nearly 300 kilometres. I preferred the openness of the road to a cramped bus any day, but in China distances were so vast it was impractical to avoid public transport completely.

The path rose and fell underneath my worn leather boots, as the trees on either side of me rustled in the darkness. There was a fluttering of small wings overhead, then more and more, until suddenly the air around me was filled with an unseen horde of bats on their way back to a nearby cave. Something else leapt from the roadside further up and sprinted into the bushes opposite, making strange chirruping noises as it crashed through the undergrowth. Soon after there came a splash of water from the same direction, and then an animal scream that was violent and short-lived.

These sounds of the wild were eventually replaced by those of the human world: a buffalo being urged on by a farmer in the fields below the road, a dog barking from behind a village fence somewhere, and voices — two men coming towards me out of the gloom. For a brief moment I considered ducking into the bushes on my left, but I decided against it after realising they were probably as aware of me as I was of them. Indeed, they had stopped talking and had slowed their pace, concentrating their attention on the figure that was coming towards them and straining their eyes to make out whether it was friend or foe.

A voice called out, 'Who's there?'

I replied with the typical greeting in Mandarin, 'Ni hao' — 'Hello.'

By now we were no more than two metres apart and I could see they were trappers, carrying large cane cages on their backs and smaller ones in each of their hands. We stopped short and sized each other up. Satisfied I wasn't the police, who might have wanted a bribe to let them keep their illicit cargo, their mood switched from defensive to curious and I soon found myself facing a barrage of questions, most of which I couldn't decipher. I told them who I was and where I was going, which is pretty much what anyone in the world wants to know when they meet a stranger, and sure enough this did the trick. In the growing light I could see them smiling and nodding. The one nearer to me offered the contents of his smallest cage. I declined and they laughed and took a few steps closer. That was when the smell hit me, the smell of wet fur and fear. Many pairs of eyes looked out from those cages, and I wondered what it would cost to buy the lot and set them free. But the two hunters were indifferent and began to move off, clearly wanting to get to the markets before sun-up, when the first buyers would arrive to barter for ingredients for that day's menu. I watched them depart, their bamboo backpacks of wildlife swaying to and fro as they walked, until the darkness swallowed them whole.

Eventually the dawn came, revealing that the road I was on skirted a thick forest of mature camphor trees and lofty bamboo, through the upper branches of which the sun's rays were now passing, sending arrows of light to the leafy forest floor below. Birds chattered noisily to one another and occasionally swooped to pluck a tasty insect in mid-air. I had the momentary impression that I was looking at a China from centuries ago, when feudal lords held sway over their fiefdoms and used private armies to defend villages and collect taxes. In the early days of Communism, Mao Tse-tung and his men ran the gauntlet of these fierce rulers, either asking for safe passage or fighting for it hand-to-hand. In later years, when Mao's control was absolute and Communism at its zenith, he exacted his revenge and reduced the feudal lords to the level of peasants. Little mercy was shown.

By midday, I had reached the village of Shengmu in Ji'an county, thanks in part to a ride on the back of a local farmer's cart. It was powered by an old tractor and was filled with bales of straw. My job was to sit on top, along with his two young sons, and keep some weight on the load. We bounced along for an hour like this, fearing the ever-present threat of potholes that might send us flying. Whenever we hit a bump, the farmer would glance over his shoulder to make sure he'd lost neither family nor foreigner nor cargo.

The village was busy with its market day. The sun shone as people from all round the countryside arrived by car, bike and donkey to buy and sell their wares, or even find a mate. My farming friend was one such type. His wife, the mother of his sons, was dead, which he communicated to me by putting his hands to his ear like a pillow of eternal sleep, and so he hoped to find another partner there. She would have to be hard working, I mused, and, judging by the smell of his breath that morning, tolerant of his love of raw onions.

I like food markets in China because it's not just food you'll find there. You'll almost certainly come upon someone with an old pedal-operated sewing machine who will mend the tear in your shirt or the hole in your bag perfectly. Just as importantly, there will be someone to shave your head or prescribe medical cures for a host of ailments. Sadly, however, like so many other markets in China, this one was also doing a roaring trade in wild animals. There were bamboo cages, like the ones I'd encountered in the night, from which creatures stared out in a display of unremitting fear or spat and yowled with terror. Mere hours ago, these creatures had been living beside a river or stream, maybe under a log. Now they were today's lunch.

It's not that I'm a vegetarian. It's just the way anything that looks even remotely edible in China soon finds itself on the national menu. Never mind the endangered species lists: when it comes to priorities, environmental concerns come a distant second to the dietary needs of the country's gargantuan population. Of course it's easy to point the finger and we in the West are not blameless, with our factory farms churning out animals for fast-food burgers. But at least we put some energy into habitat conservation and protecting wildlife. It was maddening to see such rampant consumption without thought for the consequences.

I bent down to one of the cages and found a sad-looking goose, his wings trussed up with string and his feet encased in rubber bands. He didn't protest as much as the other wild animals when I came near, as if he had long since resigned himself to his fate. A fat goose was going to make a much more attractive meal to a hungry Han, rather than some scrawny creature trapped in the forest that morning, so I figured he wouldn't have long to wait before being chosen for the chopping block. But it also struck me at that precise moment that, this time at least, I wasn't going to let it happen. I would make a statement right there and then, by ensuring that this goose stayed *un*cooked. And that is how I came to meet Errol.

The stall owner offered to behead him on the spot. I quickly said no, alive was quite okay. So she put him in a plastic bag, still tied up, with his head poking out, and I wandered through the market carrying my new buddy, not entirely sure what to do next. I could have simply let him go on the spot, but he'd have been caught again in minutes. I'd already watched another stall owner, in the act of showing off a live eel to a customer, accidentally drop it into the gutter. The poor thing swam furiously through the dirty ditch for a few metres, but there was nowhere to go. The stall owner jumped ahead and plucked it out of the flotsam and jetsam, thumped it over the head with the butt of his knife and dumped it back in the tank it had come from.

That was not going to happen to my goose. I bundled him under my arm for extra safety and retreated from the market to formulate a plan. Errol said little, except for a slightly uncertain *rronk* sound that came from deep inside his throat. I thought I'd try to find a room, but it was harder than anticipated. Few places wanted to take in a foreigner and his bird, apparently because of fire safety.

'No cooking in the room,' protested one manager.

I attempted to persuade him that I wasn't going to set fire to his hotel by cooking the bird in the middle of the room, and eventually convinced him that Errol meant more to me than a quick meal. I could stay one night, he said, but there would be an extra charge for the goose. That seemed fair enough.

On the second floor we were shown down a long hall and into a small, dingy, single room with heavy shutters that let in only scraps of light. They would only open a few centimetres, so the room smelt dank from lack of ventilation. Still, it had a separate bathroom and here I deposited Errol, who was beginning to get restless and strain at the strings that confined his movement. The poor creature deserved better and so, perhaps a little unwisely given my lack of knowledge of goose recapture techniques, I elected to pour some water into the bath and release him.

Bad idea.

As soon as the shackles were off, so too was Errol. He jumped up on the edge of the bath and hissed ferociously. His wingspan was huge and that little room suddenly felt far too small for the two of us. Gingerly, keeping a reasonably safe distance from that sharp beak and irascible temper, I exited stage right and closed the door on those glaring yellow eyes. For a moment I leant my head against the wooden door and listened, hearing nothing at first, until there came the unmistakable noise of splashing.

Downstairs, on the wall of the hotel reception was a tourist map of the surrounding area and on that map, not far outside the village, a lake was marked.

I pointed to it and asked the manager how to get there.

'Bus,' he said. Then he pointed to another sheet of paper on the wall that listed the timetable and fares. This was apparently no ordinary lake but one of the area's major scenic attractions.

'What's it called?' I asked.

He said nothing, but jabbed a bony finger at a line of English writing at the bottom of the page.

I read it out loud: 'Peaceful Lake of Mist Mountain.'

I thought of Errol, who was hopefully enjoying a leisurely swim in his bath. He'd had a tough time of late. Even if geese had as many lives as cats, then he must surely be perilously close to using up his entitlement. Perhaps he would have a better chance of survival in a place with such an enlightened name as Peaceful Lake of Mist Mountain. It might even be some kind of nature reserve — a wildlife sanctuary where he could live out the rest of his days in avian contentment.

I looked back at the manager, who was absent-mindedly brushing dandruff from his shoulders.

'Two tickets please.'

SIXTEEN

By night, the market stalls had closed and been replaced with a row of makeshift kitchens that did business under the light of a single line of fluorescent tubes. Surly folk stood around charcoal braziers, fanning the flames in order to roast skewered meat of unknown origin. I kept walking until a kitchen came into view that was selling a kind of noodle soup. The owner brought out a wooden stool for me and placed it beside a small table that rocked on the uneven cobblestones. She then produced a steaming bowl of hot liquid, which contained a few vegetables, thick strap-like noodles and some lumps of tofu. It was spicy and delicious, and smelt of fresh herbs and garlic.

Nearby was a bowl of water containing porcelain spoons that were for the exclusive use of her hungry patrons, as well as a bamboo cup filled with chopsticks. They looked cleaner, so I took a pair and, after wolfing down the noodles, slurped the watery soup direct from the bowl, leaving just a leafy green vegetable at the bottom. I pointed this out to the owner and asked if she had any more by saying 'You mei-you' in a way that I hoped imitated the correct rising and descending tones required in the Chinese language.

The owner was a rosy-cheeked Han Chinese woman of about 40, in brown slacks and white blouse, over which she wore a grease-stained apron. She looked at the contents of the bowl and, with hands on hips, barked out a command to the kitchen. Dutifully, her teenage son appeared from behind a screen with a large knife and approached the table.

'You want more noodles?' he asked in English.

'Not noodles,' I replied with a shake of my head. 'I would like some of this.' I pointed again to the leafy green vegetable at the bottom of the bowl, which looked a little like the bushy top of a celery plant.

The boy turned to his mother, said a few words and she sort of harrumphed and shrugged her shoulders. Once again the boy turned to me: 'You want cooked?'

I replied that I wanted the vegetable raw.

'It's for my friend,' I added.

This time the mother spoke: 'Where your friend?'

I told her he was in the bathroom in the hotel across the road.

'Is he sick?' she asked.

'Not really,' I replied.

'Why he no come eat?'

'He's a goose.'

At this point the conversation was beginning to become unnecessarily complicated. I just wanted any old lettuce or cabbage that would be fit for Errol to eat, so I got up and walked them both back to their kitchen area and pointed to some scraps that were littering the ground and asked if I could have those — uncooked, as they were, never mind the dressing, in a bag, if you please. They agreed, but I couldn't be sure if they really just wanted me gone. Anyone who claims to keep a wild goose in his bath might have taken leave of his senses. Foreigners were known for their odd ways, but this was indeed strange. As I took the bag of scraps, I swear she leant forward a little to smell if I'd been drinking.

Being a source of mild amusement was by no means a new experience in China. In the more remote regions I could literally just stand in one place and soon gather an audience around me, often parents with their offspring in tow. It was like being an exhibit in a circus — like the guy with two heads or the incredibly hairy man. I imagined their comments to be something like: 'Look at him, his feet are as big as Uncle Chen's prize marrows and his skin is the colour of butter beans.'

In general, however, people were reasonably polite and I sensed that parents who were pointing me out to their child were merely giving them an introduction to the wider world, a sort of impromptu lesson in European anthropology. As a Westerner in the outer provinces I was a rare breed after all, one viewed only occasionally in a book perhaps or a movie, so the general reaction was still a mix of surprise and wonder. The bravest kids would come close enough to touch me and then run away if I glared at them. It was a bit of a game, which quite often ended with smiles and laughter or, occasionally, a fearful tear or two; then we would go our separate ways or, as sometimes happened, I'd be invited to share a meal with the family — part guest, part laboratory specimen.

Back in Qinghai province, near the dusty little town of Maduo, I had befriended a family of Han Chinese who considered themselves foreigners in those parts as well, Qinghai being predominantly Tibetan. Over dinner at a local restaurant we had bonded as foreigners, although, ironically, they seemed to feel more foreign, and therefore more uncomfortable, than I did. The father, who must have been only 150 centimetres tall in his shoes, was a cellphone-tower engineer and had just arrived on a two-year contract with his wife and seven-year-old son. His task was to manage a maintenance crew of burly Tibetans, whose job it was to keep other burly Tibetans from damaging the towers. These towers were believed by some to be listening devices, through which Beijing spied on the locals. Unable to tear them down, people would throw rocks at the antennas and damage the transmitters.

I asked if his job was more like that of a PR officer, in that he had to try to explain to the locals what the towers were really for. He agreed and said he'd stumbled on a unique ruse, which was to tell his team of Tibetans that the towers were emitting high-frequency signals that scared away wolves.

'Are there any wolves in these parts,' I asked, and he smiled knowingly and said, with obvious pleasure, 'Not anymore.'

The end result was that the Tibetans had started to leave the towers alone, clearly fearing wolves more than they did central government.

As we'd sat there enjoying the meal, the man's son had continually asked his mother questions about me, which she answered patiently. The father was a little embarrassed by this and told them both off. The mother replied that I couldn't understand the conversation she was having with the boy in Mandarin, so I wouldn't mind. In all truth I hadn't minded at all, partly because the boy was asking such interesting and frank questions of his mother and thereby providing me with an insight into how very young Chinese see the outside world. Amongst other things, he wanted to know why my nose was so big and why my arms were so hairy. I must have looked like an alien to him: big, bulbous and heavy compared to his slender-boned, elf-like father.

* * *

Back in the hotel, Errol had made an unholy mess of the bathroom, spreading feathers and goose poo all over the place. It stank to high heaven and he hissed when I switched on the light, so I ended up throwing the contents of the bag into the bath and leaving him to it in the darkness. In the morning, somehow I was going to have to tie him up again, and it wasn't going to be easy. My goose-control experience was limited and I knew that the task would require either extreme ingenuity or good luck. In the end, when the sun came up and I'd managed a few fitful hours of sleep hatching a myriad of plans, I opted to employ the lace curtains from the window as a net, which I managed to throw over him to contain him. Then it was a matter of quickly trussing his wings and feet in the same way they'd been tied in the market. Once disabled, Errol became as meek as a lamb.

The journey to the lake by minibus was a meandering trip, through lush green paddy fields and orchards of kumquats drenched by recent rain, up into mountains cloaked by mist until a steep valley came into view, and then down a rutted track to the water's edge. The other passengers were a young Chinese couple on holiday with their small child, and two girls in their mid-twenties. The girls carried small, colourful daypacks emblazoned with the female rabbit cartoon character called Miffy. They also had Miffy shirts and Miffy diaries in which they wrote things down with Miffy pens.

'You know Dick Bruna?' I asked, referring to the artist who had invented the character in the 1950s.

But they didn't and so that ended the conversation. Errol was of far greater interest to them, however. They were no doubt curious as to what the Westerner was doing on the bus with a goose tied up with string and swaddled in a cheap plastic bag, and they took many photographs of Errol and me until our bus creaked to a stop in a car park surrounded by lush vegetation. There was a trail off to the left that circumnavigated the lake and the family quickly disappeared down it. The two girls followed soon after, so that, aside from the bus driver, Errol and I were alone. The driver perched on a rock, smoking a cigarette, as he watched me carry Errol down to the lake's edge. I thought I should say a few meaningful words to mark the moment, but I couldn't think of any. So, in the end, I simply untied Errol from his string and rubber bands and set him free.

First, he fell over. Then, unsteadily, he picked himself up, stretched his wings and honked noisily, sniffing the air somewhat cautiously. Possibly stunned not to find himself on a chopping block, Errol was taking his time to sample his new-found liberty. But, within a few minutes, either the blood had returned to his wingtips or he'd decided enough was enough. He had one last go at biting me then launched himself into the air and flew away, low across the lake. It felt good, I have to admit.

From over my shoulder came a cough. The driver stood nearby, stamping out his cigarette on the rough ground. He then lifted his head towards the fast-disappearing goose as if to say, 'What's all this about?'

I was in the process of trying to think up a suitable reply, using my limited Chinese, when he spoke in clear English.

'I have seen a lot of things, but that is a first. Most foreigners buy trinkets, but you — you buy a nice fat goose and then let him go.'

The driver whistled and shook his head in bewilderment, then opened his pack of Camel cigarettes and offered me one. I shook my head.

'Suit yourself,' he replied with a shrug, before pulling one out and tapping the end thoughtfully on the back of the packet.

'Your English is very good,' I said, quietly thrilled to have found someone so proficient this far off the beaten track. It struck me I could learn a lot from him.

He introduced himself as Chou and described how he'd grown up from the age of 17 in Hong Kong, working in tourism for 20-odd years before China regained the territory in 1997, ending 150 years of British colonial rule. It was a sad day, he said, when the Union Jack came down and was replaced by the red-and-yellow flag of the People's Republic of China.

'But what a party,' he said quietly.

The day of the handover it had teemed down with rain, but that had not deterred the millions of Hong Kong residents from coming out to watch all the pomp and ceremony the best of British could muster, including the Prince of Wales in full regalia. As grey army trucks filled with Chinese soldiers, standing as stiff and resolute as statues, came rumbling down through the New Territories towards Kowloon, my driver had helped organise the 25,000 fireworks that were launched from barges in the harbour into the night sky. The explosions were so fierce people in the outlying districts thought a war had started. After each salvo was fired, the barges dropped a foot into the water so that those on the decks were briefly suspended in mid-air. Then, without further ado, the royal yacht *Britannia* had steamed out of Hong Kong harbour one last time, flanked by her flotilla of British Navy ships and by fireboats that saluted her by spraying great arcs of water. A century and a half after having taken Hong Kong by force during the First Opium War in 1841, when Britain responded to the Chinese government's seizure of 1,210 tonnes of opium by sinking almost its entire navy, she quietly handed back the so-called last prize of the Empire.

'But,' Chou said softly, 'the Chinese fireworks display the next day was even greater. If there is one thing the Chinese know how to do, it is fireworks.'

I thought it was interesting that he referred to the Chinese as if he were not one of them, and when I quizzed him about whether he thought of himself as being British he laughed.

'Of course not,' he replied. 'I am Hong Kongese.'

Therein lay the truth, that Hong Kong saw itself as superior to mainland China, a separate region deserving of special rank and democratic privileges, few of which were accorded to it by the Communist Party rulers after the handover. Their promises of a 'Hong Kong ruled by Hong Kong' were soon found to be little more than a form of crowd control, a way of appeasing the masses as the new owners dug in and took over. Not surprisingly, these events were watched closely by the people of Taiwan, another territory that China had long been wooing to rejoin the motherland without losing any of its political sovereignty. However, Taiwan's answer had always been a polite refusal, followed by an immediate memo to its military to bolster its forces, just to be on the safe side.

Post 1997, Chou's new employers had come down from Beijing and everything had changed. State-operated tourism was not at all his kind of thing, so he'd packed it in and started driving buses in Jiangxi province.

'Now I own the buses,' he said with an entrepreneurial smile. I noticed a little gold glinting in that grin too, and so reasoned that business had probably been quite good to him. It turned out he had three small coaches that ferried tourists to and from the lake, mostly Han Chinese who came to stretch their legs and visit a famous grotto on the far side. Mao was said to have sheltered in it when he was on the run from the Nationalists, but it was better known for a natural spring that bubbled up out of its floor. This was said to promise long life, prosperity and healthy offspring to those who drank from it.

'Do you believe it?' I queried.

He shrugged his shoulders again. 'Well, it worked for Mao Tse-tung didn't it?'

'Long life, yes. Prosperity, maybe. But what about his children?' I asked, steering the conversation purposefully.

'Mao was the father of China,' he said. 'I don't think he had much time for his own children.'

Chou angled his head and blew a puff of smoke skywards

through the corner of his mouth. He then said something that stopped me in my tracks.

'You know the story of his first son, Mao An Hong?'

'It's the reason I'm here talking to you now,' I replied.

'How's that?' he asked, suddenly quite serious.

'I'm looking for him,' I said.

'Why? Does he owe you money?'

I laughed. 'No, not at all. It's purely out of curiosity. I came here to search for some answers.'

'In that case,' he replied. 'This is your lucky day.'

Chou gestured for me to follow him back to the minibus and, when we got there, he reached into the glove compartment and pulled out a thick notebook filled with writing. On a blank page he scribbled a name and a phone number, then he tore out the page and handed it to me.

'This is my friend; he's a journalist. Like you he went looking for Mao An Hong. He wrote an article about it for his newspaper, but after it was printed he got into trouble — a lot of trouble. The authorities …' he said ominously, pausing to look at me before finishing, '… if you know what I mean.'

Apparently, the piece of paper in my hand bore the name and phone number of the man who had first sprung to light back in Chengdu, when Dale, the friendly American academic, had gone through his university's files for me. It seemed incredible in a country this size that such a random meeting could result in such a connection, but I wasn't about to question my good fortune. In fact I was rejoicing in it when the driver tapped the page.

'He's south of here, in Ruijin. You'd better hurry though,' he warned.

'Why?'

'He has the cancer. I haven't seen or heard from him in months. For all I know he might already be dead.'

From across the lake came the sound of two gunshots that echoed back and forth against the hillsides for so long that it sounded like a battle was being waged between forces on either side. Immediately I thought of Errol and wondered if he was safe. And sure enough, when the Miffy twins turned up an hour later, along with the young couple dragging their tired and screaming toddler, they were followed by a lone hunter with a shotgun in his hand and a limp white bird slung over one shoulder.

He was young, cocky and full of himself. He boarded the minibus and sat across the aisle from me the whole way back, his bloody kill carelessly thrown on the floor beneath his seat. Worse still, he wanted to learn some English.

He shouted to Chou: 'Hey driver. Ask the Big Nose foreigner, how do I ask my girlfriend to marry me?'

'He wants you to tell him how to propose in English,' translated Chou.

'Oh that's easy,' I said. 'Happy to help.'

Slowly and clearly, so that he would have no trouble remembering this one sentence for the rest of his miserable life, I enunciated to the hunter, 'I … am … an … arse … hole.'

As we drove back through the mountains, the hunter repeated to himself cheerfully, over and over, 'I am an arse-hole … I am an arse-hole …'

Errol was as dead as a doornail, but his beak hung open in a wry smile.

SEVENTEEN

That night I was on a bus to Ruijin, following my route south as fast as possible. Ruijin was the first established centre of Chinese Communist power in the late 1920s, when Mao and his followers fled there from Chiang Kai-shek, taking advantage of its isolated position amidst the rugged mountains bordering Jiangxi and Fujian provinces. It was also one of the recognised starting points of the Long March in 1934, and wasn't far from Yudu, where Mao An Hong had last been seen.

The headlights lit the way in front for kilometre after kilometre, until sleep mercifully overcame me for the rest of the journey. The next I remember I was being shaken in the dark by someone and then shooed out onto a wide street already busy with men pulling large wooden handcarts laden with fresh vegetables. It was still hours before dawn.

Somewhere out there was an ailing journalist, or a dead one. Either way, I had to find a bed first of all. As usual there were several cheap ones in the vicinity of the bus station. I booked into the nearest one, paid in advance and stowed the few things I was carrying in the single room.

My chief concern was getting to a phone as soon as possible. Ruijin wasn't a big place, but it was a town nonetheless; so it had a central post office with private phone booths, from which I could call the number I'd been given. Unfortunately the person who picked up the phone at the other end couldn't make sense of my Chinese, or didn't want to, and kept hanging up. Stuck to the wall in my booth were various notices in Chinese, including one that advertised a private English-language school. I rang that number and spoke to a young-sounding girl by the name of Xu Qing, who was almost breathless in her excitement at having a native English speaker on the phone.

'We, er, I, um, don't have opportunity like this to be speaking with you,' she said sweetly.

We arranged to meet at midday on a local bridge spanning the Mianshui River, just a short distance from the central markets. When I arrived it was teeming with teenagers in smart school uniforms cycling past on old Chinese bikes, in a hurry to get home for lunch. One of them turned out to be Xu Qing.

She was 17 and in her last year of school, studying like mad to get the necessary grades for a shot at one of the better universities. The rest of her life hinged upon this success, she said. Her parents had invested every last yuan in her future. To fail would be to fail them as well.

'No pressure then,' I said jokingly, and then regretted it when this clearly struck a nerve. There was every bit of pressure, she replied. Nothing in her whole short life mattered more than getting those A grades later in the year.

'So,' I said, 'are you confident?'

'Very,' she smiled, before adding, 'except for English.'

'Hey, you're good,' I protested. But she shook her head and told me there were many who were better at conversation. That's why she was teaching English in her spare time, in order to practise what she most needed to know. It wasn't ideal though. Her students were often either very young children or businessmen with limited linguistic skills.

'So I am very happy to meet you,' she said, jumping on the spot a little.

* * *

As we walked through the markets, I explained what I needed, then showed her the name and number on the paper.

'Wang Qiushe,' she read, before reeling off the phone number. 'He is a journalist?'

'Is or was, I'm not sure.'

In a few minutes we were back at the post office and in the same phone booth as before. I pointed out her homemade sign amongst the others, then watched as she quickly scanned these before looking away embarrassed. These other signs were obviously advertising an entirely different service.

'Prostitutes,' she said a little coyly. 'I …'

I interrupted her, suddenly realising she might think I wanted more from her than help finding the journalist.

'Let's just speak to Wang,' I said apologetically.

She immediately brightened up and dialled the number. What followed was a long conversation in which Xu Qing sounded quite forceful, and yet polite, as though she were speaking with someone beneath her in life's social ranking. Midway through

Xu Qing at her school, Ruijin

she took out a pen and paper from her schoolbag and made some rough notes. There followed a lot of nodding and sounds of agreement before the phone was put back on its cradle.

'So,' she said, mentally arranging the facts. 'Wang Qiushe is in Ruijin Hospital, but he has cancer of the ...' She felt her neck with her fingers.

'Throat?'

'Yes, the throat — and cannot speak. His mother has given us permission to visit him though. She will organise it with the hospital for noon tomorrow.'

'You did all that with one call? You're incredible, Xu Qing.'

'I told her you were an important Western journalist from a large international news organisation,' she said, rather guiltily.

'Which one?'

'Oh. Just the BBC.'

Somewhat ironically, it wasn't the first time I had ended up using the BBC as a cover. In Afghanistan, a group of Hezbollah had incorrectly assumed the same and had therefore been willing to smuggle me across the border from Iran. When I'd found out their mistake, it had been too late to tell them and so I'd just gone along with it.

'So, what now?' I asked.

'I'm late for class, but I will meet you at the bridge tomorrow. It's a holiday, so no school.'

With that, she smiled and ran out the post office door trailing her schoolbag. But before going much further, she stopped and looked back.

'Would you like to come with me?'

It took me all of two seconds to decide and say yes.

* * *

Xu Qing's school was in a built-up area surrounded by high walls and security guards who checked my shoulder bag before letting me through. Her next class was Chemistry and the room was upstairs along an exterior walkway. We passed other classrooms where students had their heads down on their tables, sleeping.

'Xu Qing,' I called out, as we half walked, half ran past her startled schoolmates on the walkway. 'You're bound to do better in your grades than these guys, they're not even awake in class!'

'Silly. Class hasn't started yet. They're just napping like cats.'

She then described a school day that began at seven in the morning, went through to midday, started again at 2 p.m. and ran until 5 p.m. then resumed after dinner for further study from 7 p.m. to 10 p.m. My kids had it easy by comparison, I told her.

'Really?' she said. 'What times do they study?'

'From 9 a.m. until 3 p.m., with an hour off for lunch.'

She laughed. 'In a month when the exams are closer, that's our normal weekend.'

My arrival in Chemistry unwittingly caused a chain reaction. Sleepy heads popped up from their resting places one after the other, as the class took note of Xu Qing's new friend. Soon the female teacher was having a hard time getting everyone seated. I apologised for arriving unannounced and offered to leave at once, but she insisted I stay. Indeed she let me take over half her class time with a not-so-brief rundown on where I was from and what I was doing in China — and at Ruijin State High School. When it came to fielding a question about Chemistry, however, I gave up and ruefully took a seat at the back to listen until the bell went.

It was fascinating to watch these typical Chinese students work with such determination to succeed. But I couldn't help but wonder what kind of person would develop from such a gruelling routine and potentially suffocating parental expectations. Then again, how would my children hope to compete on the job market if they were to come across a horde of workaholic, highly motivated Chinese? As always, when China sets its mind to doing something, it is done on a grand scale, which in turn gives it enormous momentum. On the other hand, was our quieter, more easygoing way of doing things going to produce happier, more well-rounded individuals? In my mind I flicked through the stories I'd read of Asian students finding the pressure too much and taking their lives. In China, suicide is the fifth leading cause of death, and the leading one amongst the young. The country's huge population means the statistics always seem overblown but, nonetheless, an estimated 287,000 people kill themselves annually — one every two minutes. Ten times that number are unsuccessful attempts. That puts China near the top of the world's national suicide rate table.

It's all very well to try to produce armies of talented teenagers, but at what cost? And of course, whereas in the West youngsters usually have brothers and sisters to lean on as well as their parents, kids like Xu Qing are usually only children, part of the 'Little Emperor' generation created by China's 'one-child' rule. Moreover, their mothers and fathers work so slavishly to bring in the money needed to pay for the best education that they are not always available to their children. Grandparents are often entrusted with the role of counsellor, but there is no question on which an 80-year-old can offer any wise words that would be relevant to a teen.

Later, after school was finished for the week and night had fallen, Xu Qing and a few of her classmates, still in their navy blue and white-shirt uniforms, took me to a KFC for dinner. The group included Dong, who looked like an Asian popstar in his mirror shades, plus Huang and Chang, two pretty girls. It was Dong's birthday and we sang 'Happy Birthday' to him in the time-honoured tune. I asked if this was normal and Chang said 'Of course', but she didn't know where or how the tune had originated. I suggested they Google it and no one had heard of that name either. China, it seemed, had its own state-controlled search engine, called Baidu. I'd never heard of that and made a mental note to look it up when I got home.

'So what do you guys do in your spare time?' I asked.

They looked at each other, seeing who was going to go first.

'Computer games,' proffered Dong eventually. He was definitely the coolest of the group.

'Computer games also,' said Chang, who was clearly trying to impress Dong.

Huang chipped in enthusiastically as well: 'Me too.'

Chang dropped her jaw in disgust, as if to say 'Since when?', and Dong did his best not to notice.

Xu Qing stayed well out of it. She had no time for adolescent games. She was all business.

'If I can get into a big university, I'd like to be a writer too,' she said, gesturing towards me.

'What would you write?'

'Romantic fiction.'

Huang put her hand to her mouth to hide a smirk. Xu Qing gave her a withering sideways glare and hit back immediately:

'About a girl who loves a boy, who loves someone else.'

She looked pointedly at Dong, then at Huang.

Ouch, I thought. Xu Qing wasn't messing around. I noticed Chang was the one smiling now, although the 'boy' in question was still admiring his reflection in the glass of the restaurant.

Huang got up and went to the bathroom in a huff, while Chang did her best to get Dong's attention. It was going to be a challenge. Clearly Dong fancied Dong more than anyone else.

'Well,' I said, 'good luck with that. It's not an easy job. Are there many established romance authors already in China?'

'Zhang Xiao San. I like her books. The women in her stories are strong and independent. They want equality in love,' she announced in a voice raised a notch above its normal sweet tone.

'What about you?' I asked. 'Do you have a boyfriend?'

Xu Qing glanced in Dong's direction and, so that the others couldn't hear, leant forward across the table, moving her plate of chicken nuggets to one side with the back of her hand.

'I don't like boys,' she whispered matter-of-factly. 'When I am ready, I will take a man.'

She pushed the plate in my direction.

'Nugget?' she asked.

Xu Qing was becoming a force to be reckoned with. But then Chinese women are often in the driving seat when it comes to relationships, and more besides. If Mao's Communism had achieved anything for women in the twenty-first century, it had helped them break free of the shackles of chauvinism. Indeed, before Mao, women were taught obedience to men and were not allowed to occupy prominent positions in community or political groups. Following the Revolution, however, all that changed, and suddenly women's groups sprang up to denounce the old thinking and carve out a new place alongside their male counterparts, rather than beneath them.

Slightly fortuitously, a refreshed Huang returned just then and the group decided to go and hang out by the local fountain, which had been decorated with colourful underwater lights for the Mid-Autumn Moon Festival. This is a time when families get together and, as a result, the town was busy with parents fussing over their only children. I grinned at one such kid and she promptly started screaming in terror.

What was she seeing? A Western devil, a thing of nightmares to come? Was I stirring up trouble with my very presence?

'I think it's time I went,' I proposed.

'You're trouble,' Xu Qing smiled, with eyes that twinkled just a little too mischievously.

We retreated and found a quiet place to sit and talk. Dong had suddenly developed an interest in things other than his perfectly coiffed image, and started up a conversation about cars. He wanted to know if I had seen the new Lamborghini, a car that could do 0–100 kilometres per hour in 3.4 seconds, he said. The girls rolled their eyes, but he wasn't about to give up.

'One day I will drive across China in one,' he boasted, adjusting his sunglasses so that they perched on the end of his nose before coolly pushing them back again with his middle finger. I told him he might need a Land Rover rather than an Italian sportscar, as beyond Gansu province — a halfway point of sorts for his intrepid journey — there were few main roads as such. The idea that the rest of China might not be as civilised as the part he lived in perplexed him greatly. He'd never been outside Ruijin before.

'You've been there?' he asked.

'Yes. Qinghai, Gansu, Xinjiang. In fact you might find even the Land Rover a bit useless in the Taklimakan Desert. Camels are better there.'

The ridiculous thought of Dong on a camel made the girls squeal with delight. For a moment his veneer of sophistication weakened, but then his confidence returned anew when I said he could be something of a Lawrence of Arabia figure, swathed in white, flowing robes and with a curved sword in his belt.

He nodded in a suave manner as he smiled.

'I like,' he said finally. 'Have you ridden a camel?'

'A long time ago,' I replied. 'They're uncomfortable, noisy, disgusting animals that will spit in your face if you're not careful, but there is no better beast of burden for crossing the sandy wastelands of western China. Cheaper than a Lamborghini too.'

The idea of spitting camels seemed to spoil Dong's romantic notion of travel and the conversation then took an off-road detour of its own as the girls started to ask about my life — who was I married to, for example.

'Libby is a classical pianist and music teacher,' I said.

This really impressed them, to the point that they huddled in closer to hear more. I described her lovely blue eyes and blonde hair and how I was the luckiest man alive to be with someone as beautiful as she.

'When she plays, people passing in the street sometimes stop outside our house to listen.'

The girls thought this was amazing, a world away from their own lives, as indeed it was. Looking around at the multitude of people who packed the small square, and at the eager faces of Xu Qing and her friends, I did feel a little homesick. I'd come so far and travelled so many thousands of kilometres over such a long time, and part of me yearned to be done with this madness, this insanely ambitious journey. Compared to my quest, the idea of Dong crossing China in a Lamborghini didn't seem so far-fetched after all.

Nevertheless, things were looking up. I was feeling more than optimistic.

'You know what?' I said to Dong.

'What?'

'Go get your Lamborghini. Start driving west and don't look back.'

Dong rose theatrically to his feet and punched the air.

'Yeah!' he proclaimed. 'The Asian Lawrence of Arabia.'

Huang and Chang swooned with unbridled teenage delight.

EIGHTEEN

Ward Three of the Ruijin People's Hospital was thronging with orderlies in blue smocks and well-dressed visitors carrying Moon cakes. Tethered to a mobile intravenous drip, a bare-chested geriatric patient looked on, with a fag in his mouth.

I found the room we were looking for and opened the door quietly. Inside were six beds; all were empty save for one. By the window lay our journalist, seemingly dozing, with a small blackboard on his chest on which he'd been writing. His neck was swathed in bandages and he looked awful. For a moment I thought we should leave him be, but Xu Qing tugged at his pyjama sleeve and he came to with a start.

Wang Qiushe had aged considerably and looked quite different from the photograph I had seen. His cheekbones protruded from his face and his eyes had burrowed into their sockets, as if they were trying to hide. Despite his ill health, however, he still managed to smile and greet us with a nod of his head, as if we'd just popped by his house for a glass of tea. I carried two wooden chairs over and placed one on either side of his bed. Xu Qing made the introductions and explained why we were there, based on the detailed briefing I had given her, and while she spoke his eyes looked me up and down.

'Xu Qing,' I asked once she'd finished, 'can you ask him what he knows about Mao An Hong?'

Wang listened to Xu Qing then picked up his blackboard and, with a piece of chalk, wrote a few characters in Chinese with a shaky hand. It seemed like an age before she could read his answer.

'Dead,' she said sadly.

Wang rubbed the characters out with his pyjama sleeve and continued writing, as Xu Qing translated.

'Killed … by … police … in Ganzhou.'

'When?' I asked, trying to swallow the disappointment I was now feeling.

Wang's chalk moved again, this time with greater urgency. Then his arm dropped to his side after the exertion.

'Long, long ago,' read Xu Qing.

She looked at me sympathetically and said, 'I'm sorry.'

'So let me get this straight. What he is saying is that the son of Mao was murdered by police forces — which doesn't make much sense to me because the police would have been loyal Maoists — and that this happened some time back?'

She shrugged her shoulders and looked at Wang, who was writing again.

'I can't believe it,' I said. 'If it were true, surely someone would have known about this? It would have been global news, and I don't think even the Chinese government could have swept something that big under the carpet.'

'He says ask Zhou Fung Mu.'

'Who's he?'

As if expecting my question Wang was already writing the answer. We waited patiently. The chalk was nearly all gone and he had to hold what little remained with his fingertips.

'Ganzhou Chief of Police,' said Xu Qing finally.

Wang sighed and sank deeper into his pillows, as if a great weight had been lifted from him. He closed his eyes, but this time they didn't open again. His breathing was shallow and laboured. I felt guilty that we had used up so much of his precious energy. Down the corridor I could hear the metallic rattle of an orderly's trolley approaching.

'Perhaps we should go,' Xu Qing said.

I nodded, but as I got up from the chair it made a scratching noise against the floor and Wang's eyes flicked open. His hand grabbed mine and squeezed, then with a chalk-stained finger he drew lines on the crisp white sheet that covered him.

Xu Qing followed each line and then looked puzzled.

'What did he write?' I asked.

Outside the orderly was singing; her voice was shrill and off-key. She came round the corner to find us both standing beside Wang's frail body. Her song ended abruptly, mid-note.

'Xiaoxin,' muttered Xu Qing. 'It means, be careful.'

NINETEEN

The men squatted in a tight circle under a large poster of a woman advertising face cream. It was hot, even though the sun was past its zenith; a thick haze hung over everything and the hoarding provided the only welcome shade. The men wore baggy green trousers and long-sleeved shirts. The soles of their feet were cracked around the edges, especially at the heels, which bore deep fissures. In the street their carts were parked one behind the other, like cabs at a taxi rank.

Xu Qing walked beside me saying nothing. I noticed how much older she looked out of her school clothes. The men ogled my pretty dark-haired companion in her short skirt and T-shirt as they smoked cheap cigarettes and waited for their next delivery job. She quickened her step until we were well past.

'What will you do now?' she asked.

'Go to Ganzhou, I guess. Maybe see if I can find out anything more about this man.'

'Zhou Fung Mu?'

'Yes,' I said. 'Perhaps there's more to the story.'

We walked on a little more before she spoke again.

'In Zhang Xiao San's book *Song in the Clouds*, there are

times when I think the story is over for the main character, Huo Yunge. But then in the next chapter it begins again and I am happy for her.'

'What happens in the end?'

'She marries a handsome prince.'

'Good,' I said.

'No, not good,' she replied. 'He's the wrong prince. She actually wants to marry the emperor.'

'So that's that?'

'No, she has great ambitions. She doesn't give up. Huo Yunge becomes a powerful woman in the emperor's court and *then* she marries her true love.'

'Okay,' I said. The last thing I needed right now was a discourse on the highs and lows of Xu Qing's favourite romance novel.

'So you see,' she continued, 'her story is just like yours.'

'Come again?'

Xu Qing skipped along in front of me then turned round, spreading her arms out wide.

'She doesn't give up of course.'

Maybe, despite her youthful exuberance, she had a point. After such a promising trail had gone cold, I was down, but not completely out. There was still something of a mystery surrounding Wang's version of events. Had he been well enough to speak, who knows what else he might have told us. It could be that I was still close to finding out the truth.

When I told Xu Qing that I would leave the next day for Ganzhou she was upset. Apparently she and her friends had been hoping to take me to Ruijin's most famous historic site.

'Is it far?' I asked.

'No, the Red Well is close,' she said. 'My friends have arranged transport for all of us to go.'

Xu Qing wasn't taking no for an answer.

'Be at the bridge at nine o'clock tomorrow morning,' she said. Then she kicked up her heels and ran off down a side street, in the direction of her home.

* * *

That night I found a cool alleyway filled with the wood smoke emanating from several family-run kitchens. Assorted wooden tables with miscellaneous chairs had been spread out on the pavement under fluorescent lights and all were occupied by locals or visiting workers. I waited for a while until a table became available and then sat down. No sooner had I done so than a family also moved in. Suddenly, I was the surprise guest rubbing shoulders with Mum, Dad, Granny, Grandpa and a little boy about two years old. He sat on his father's knee and seemed none too phased about me being there. They ordered without even looking at the menu and, when they saw me trying to decipher its two creased laminated pages, they chose for me as well, including a few bottles of Chinese beer. Everyone laughed when I taught the small boy to say, 'Hello, how are you?' and 'What's your name?', though Mum had had enough after the millionth repeat and then made him sit still so that the others could talk. Even though no English was spoken, I was made to feel part of every conversation. Tales were told and, once the effects of the beer took hold, songs were sung. The father wrote the lyrics of one beautiful tune on some paper and I had it translated later, though it's clear the translator wasn't quite up to the task:

> *Don't, my love, be jealous of the flower*
> *your sweat glands perspire great beauty*
> *Don't, my love, be jealous of the mountain*
> *Your sweet voice is high like the cliff*
> *That I leap from when you come near*
> *Leave regret for your next life*
>
> *Don't, my love, be envious of the sun*
> *your eyes are like a burnt-out fuse*
> *Don't, my love, be envious of the ocean*
> *you're as fat as all the water*
> *in every stream and every sea*
> *Leave regret for your next life*
>
> *Don't, my love, resent the trees*
> *Your spirit is as strong as wood*
> *Don't, my love, resent the moon*
> *Your skin shines like an oil lamp*
> *to light the way for this weary heart*
> *Leave regret for your next life*

The inclusion of terms such as 'sweat glands' and 'oil lamp' in a love song might be questionable, but it still sounded great. And it turned out to be nothing short of a brilliant night out. The family tolerated my gradually improving Mandarin and taught me some new words, all of which went into my journal.

For me, language is an easy thing to learn phonetically, from a real person. Textbooks I find difficult and laborious to wade through, but give me a pen and some paper and I'm happy collecting words and phrases to add to my vocabulary. It's being *in situ* that really helps me get to grips with a language. But then, take me out of the country and a few months later its language will be mixed up with other ones I've acquired over the years. German is now fused with Persian, French with Pashtu. Because of its wildly different nuances Mandarin survived longer, but it too eventually became a muddle. Despite this, and to my amazement, I can return to a country and, within days or even hours of being back, the correct words slip back into focus. The mind never ceases to amaze.

We shared the plates of food and drank endless cups of green tea, until junior yawned and it was time to go. I didn't pay — they wouldn't let me. It was particularly generous, as it was patently obvious that the father and mother weren't big earners working in some flash office. Judging by the man's hands, he probably cleaned or worked a machine. Just like his father and his father before him, probably. Yet they still insisted on treating me to a bowl of noodles.

It made me wonder about Xu Qing and her family. I got the impression they would be just like these hard-working people. In Xu Qing's parents' case, they were pinning all their hopes on their daughter to improve their situation. As I walked back to the hotel, I wondered what I could do to help her — and her loved ones — get ahead in life.

* * *

Early in the morning I got up, showered in the bathroom down the hall, put on the clean clothes I had washed in the sink the previous night, and walked the short distance to the bridge. In June 1934, 86,000 Communist troops under the command of Fang Zhimin had used the same bridge to cross the Mianshui River and eventually hurl themselves at a very surprised Nationalist army to the north, which was vastly superior in number at the time and did not expect an attack on its heavily fortified 'turtle-shell' perimeter. With fire coming from all directions the Communists were wiped out. Yet in one sense they were entirely successful. Chiang Kai-shek was fooled into thinking they would attack again at this point, and so brought in even more troops from neighbouring units manning his blockhouse lines. It proved to be a mistake, and was just the opportunity Mao's First Army needed to escape.

On 16 October 1934, Mao made the arrangements for his son to be left behind with his own younger brother, Mao Zetan, then ordered a Communist army of about 130,000 to attack Chiang Kai-shek's weakened defensive blockade to the west, near Yudu. The vast majority, including Mao and He Zizhen, made it through the lines; about 30,000 troops stayed behind to fight, amongst them Mao Zetan.

Having given Mao the chance to get away, many of these Communists simply melted away into the countryside, though several prominent leaders of this rearguard action were captured and executed by the Nationalists after the fall of Ruijin six months later, including Mao Zetan — the last-known person to have seen Mao An Hong alive.

The market was already in full swing and I bought a bag of fruit to share, thinking there'd be a car or bus along any minute.

But the vehicle that turned up a short while later wasn't quite what I'd expected. This one had two wheels, was two sizes too small for me and had a spring poking out of its seat.

Xu Qing's friends arrived like the Famous Five, on bikes of every description, ready for an adventure. Xu Qing hopped off and explained that, if I pedalled, she'd sit on the rack at the back.

'You can ride a bicycle, yes?' she asked with a note of concern.

I'd ridden road bikes hundreds of kilometres in a single day and raced mountain bikes over the toughest terrain, so the prospect of the day's ride didn't perturb me in the least — apart from the errant steel spring in the seat. This was remedied when Xu Qing tied one of her old school textbooks on top of it. So, thanks to *Applied Mathematics*, we were off — albeit without lashings and lashings of ginger beer.

The route we took was through the town and out past an industrial district that wasn't showing much industry. Grass grew up through cracks in the road and on the footpaths, making the place seem like a ghost town. High fences guarded concrete grain silos that were stained with rust marks, while, opposite, fields of fallow ground awaited planting. From directly behind me, Xu Qing explained:

'The factory is very modern — built by German men. But there was an argument over money and the Germans refused to teach us how to work the robots.'

'So what now?' I asked, turning my head so that she could hear.

'Nothing,' she replied. 'We wait. We Chinese are good at that.'

This reminded me of something Mao Tse-tung had apparently said (though it was also attributed to his second-in-command, Zhou Enlai) to President Nixon in 1972, when asked if he thought the French Revolution had had an impact on modern-day France. His answer, 'It is too early to tell', reflected the long-term view the Chinese take of life.

Dong, Chang and Huang led the way past fields for some distance until we came to a flat, open area dotted with a few traditional houses with walls of packed earth, painted in a weathered red ochre. The roofs were made of grey tiles and had very little pitch, giving the buildings a squashed look, and there was no sign of the gentle architectural curve that typically ran from the peak of a roof down to each corner. There were few windows and some of the walls bore large spray-painted Chinese characters. The houses looked rustic, but unfriendly.

A little further on, we reached the Red Well. There was a gate in an iron fence that was guarded by a petite woman in full Red Army costume: sky blue trousers, matching long-sleeved shirt and a cap emblazoned with a red star above the peak. She wore a black leather belt around her waist that made it look impossibly small.

I bought a ticket while the others, being students, went in for free. Aside from the well, which was made of stone, raised by about 30 centimetres and surrounded by a low, red timber fence, there was not much else to get excited about. Someone had left behind a red bucket tied to a length of rope, presumably so that visitors could quench their thirst. But when Dong offered the girls a sip of the water, they turned up their noses and screwed up their faces. Nevertheless, the aura of this austere historical relic was not lost on our party. It was here, they said with a note of reverence, that the first Communist government was formed, that Mao and Zhou Enlai held court and manifestos were created. There was even a mint, which printed the first Communist currency. Of course, that was all before the Nationalist army chased them out on the Long March and burnt everything to the ground. Only the well survived.

'What about these other buildings?' I asked quizzically.

'New,' said Dong, waving an arm out across the area. 'All new. But made to look old.'

The ticket afforded us entry to some of the houses, which were meagrely decorated in the extreme. The recurring arrangement in most rooms was a simple wooden chair tucked under a small, roughly sawn timber desk beneath a window with, in some cases, a low bench or a single bed, its wooden slats covered by a straw-stuffed mattress, against a wall. The minimalism could have been due to budget constraints on the set designers, or it could in fact have been an accurate representation of the period — or perhaps both. Either way, because we knew the pieces weren't genuine, the overall impression was a little flat. Like some of China's Long March history, the display had clearly been re-created to fit with the accepted version of events.

We cycled back the way we'd come, eating the fruit I'd bought at the market, while Xu Qing sang patriotic songs and giggled. The others joined in and taught me the first words of a revolutionary song, 'The Sky Above the Liberated Zone', which joyfully praised the unity of the people under the red flag of the Chinese Communist Party.

A young woman keeps cool
on the back of a bicycle

When that ended, I said, without trying to be funny, 'Give us another song, Dong.'

Xu Qing chortled, then poked me in the ribs.

'You're trouble,' she said.

Dong didn't get the joke, however. He started singing a more modern ballad. I asked her what it was and she explained it was the theme tune to a well-known computer game. Huang came alongside us and said in a loud voice, so that Dong could hear, 'I love computer games.'

Chang sneered and gripped her handlebars tightly.

TWENTY

Before leaving Ruijin, I asked Xu Qing if there was anything I could do to help her, aside from paying her a fee for acting as my translator. More than anything, she said, she wanted conversation. So we exchanged email addresses and promised to keep in touch. It seemed insignificant at the time, and a little miserly on my behalf, but something told me this one small gesture would have greater significance later on.

The seat next to me on the bus was filled by a short, stocky woman who clutched her canvas bags about her as if I was threatening to steal them. After half an hour it was all too much for her and she retreated to the back, preferring the discomfort of a seat above the rear suspension, which was like sitting on a trampoline, to the threat of my thievery. This meant, however, that I could stretch out a little — though not for long.

The next passenger to join me wore a grey pressed suit and carried a briefcase of black faux leather. His hair was neatly parted and seemed weighed down by something other than gravity — hair cream, perhaps. He put down the case and sat beside me.

'You are going to Ganzhou?'

'Yes. You also?'

'Inshallah.'

He was in his late twenties and a Turkic Muslim from Xinjiang. Unlike those of the more slightly built Han Chinese, his arms and thighs were thick and stretched the fabric of his suit. He smelt of aftershave and garlic, a combination that, in this heat, was most pungent. I rummaged in my pockets and found a roll of mints.

'For you,' I said.

He took one and I gestured for him to take more.

'I have plenty,' I lied.

'Tesekkur,' he said — 'thank you' in Turkish.

Tong was a specialist in sanitation, on his way to a conference in a big hotel. Normally he would have flown, but Ruijin's airport was closed. I asked him why he had a Chinese surname and he told me his mother was Uighur and his father was from Shanghai. Mixed marriages would have been almost unheard of 30 years earlier, but now the richer, better-educated Han were taking a fancy to the pretty Turkic girls, with their fine white skin. Tong's mother had left home at 19 and travelled to the big eastern cities looking for work, but found love instead.

'So you speak Turkish, Chinese and English,' I exclaimed.

'German too,' he smiled, rolling the mints around in his mouth and smoothing down the lapels of his jacket. 'Turkish is for family, Chinese for living and German is for business.'

'What about English?'

'That's for travelling the world. Anywhere you go, all hookers speak it.'

The bus hit a pothole and the people in the back shrieked as they launched into the air. Tong leant in closer and pointed at me with a finger that bore a gold ring.

'Have you been to the South Pacific?'

'A few times.'

'Ah, I saw on TV, right now there are thousands of sperm whales swimming past the islands. Why is it that they are called sperm whales? I know, is it because they have … ?'

He curved both arms out in front of him, as if he was holding a large barrel on his lap, and then laughed at his own joke. All I could think of was that nine hours squeezed between Tong and the window was going to be hard work, but after a while he excused himself and dozed off.

I lapsed in and out of sleep as well. Once I woke to see a horrible devil's face reflected in the window glass. Children's voices within the bus punctuated the constant rumble of rubber on road. Next moment the mask was removed and a boy's face smiled angelically.

We stopped to eat fried noodles at a food stall on the side of the road, beneath tarpaulins held up by bamboo poles. When it grew dark, kerosene lamps were lit and hung from wires overhead, casting an eerie yellow light over our weary group. Tong went off to pray somewhere quiet and returned seemingly refreshed, as if the act of prayer had washed him clean. Families talked together in hushed tones, strangers kept to themselves and everyone, no matter who they were, watched and waited for the driver to finish his meal and signal that it was time to board again.

Back on the bus, Tong soon grew bored. He had struck on the idea that we should become good friends and he invited me to join him at his hotel in Ganzhou. We would eat and drink together, and when he wasn't at the conference he would show me the ancient walls of the city.

'They are quite magnificent,' he said. 'Twenty feet thick in places.'

I agreed only so that he might let me rest some more.

When we eventually arrived at Ganzhou late that night, he grabbed my bag and ushered me into a waiting taxi. The hotel was five-star, he boasted.

'Best prostitutes in Jiangxi province.'

Actually the hotel was nice and my room, blissfully on a different floor from Tong's, was the best I'd seen in China. It even had Internet, cable TV and an en suite bathroom. I lay on the bed and pondered my next move. On a piece of paper in my pocket was the name of a man in Ganzhou who, according to Wang, knew the truth about Mao's son. Finding one man in a city of eight million was going to be challenging, but I also knew he was linked to the police in some way. That narrowed the field massively, surely. If I could persuade Tong to do some ringing around for me, perhaps Zhou Fung Mu might not be so hard to track down.

I put the proposal to him over breakfast the next morning and he almost choked on his tea.

'Talk to the police?'

'It's just a phone call.'

'In China, that's not a good idea.'

'Why?'

'You ask questions of them, they start asking questions of you. And when they ask questions you'd better have the answers.'

'I'll pay,' I said, putting things on a business footing I knew he'd understand. 'Name your price.'

Tong drained the remnants of the soup from his bowl and fished out an errant piece of food from his teeth. He glanced up at a clock above a fish tank filled with lobsters, before his gaze drifted further to the main foyer.

'See her?' he asked.

I looked and saw a strikingly attractive woman in a dark pencil suit, sitting by herself.

'You buy me her and we have a deal. Two phone calls.'

'I can't buy this woman,' I protested.

'She's a prostitute. Of course you can. You'll just be buying her for me.' Tong grinned and held out his hand to shake on it.

I paused. This was verging on the bizarre. I hoped my wife would understand.

'Eight phone calls,' I said.

'Three,' he countered.

'Seven. Last offer.'

'Four.'

'Six. Take it or leave it.'

'Five.'

'Done.'

We shook hands. His conference started soon after, but he'd be free in the afternoon to fulfil his end of the bargain. At night he'd collect payment, he said. Room 402. In my effort to get things moving, I'd been unwittingly transformed into a high-class pimp.

After tidying myself up a little, I sat down opposite the woman on a large black sofa and picked out a Chinese magazine from the rack. She paid little attention to me, as with her slender fingers she flicked through the emails on her phone. For a moment I began to think Tong had been wrong in his estimation of her profession, in which case I was about to get a slap in the face. I turned the page of the magazine and coughed loudly, but still got no response. I started to hum a tune and realised it was a song from *The Sound of Music*. Hardly appropriate in the circumstances, but nonetheless effective: she looked me dead in the eye and smiled.

'Hot,' I said, glancing towards the doors leading outside and using the magazine as a fan.

She glanced that way also and replied in Mandarin that tomorrow could be hotter still.

'Rain?' I suggested.

She gave me a look that said she thought a light shower was possible. I was doing famously. Temperature, precipitation — great conversation topics for finding out if a woman is on the make or not.

I was desperately trying to think up a tactful way to broach the subject of her social calendar when she beat me to it. Leaning forward she slipped her card across the table between us. On it was a black silhouette of a woman in thigh-high boots holding a whip. The trailing end curled at her stilettoed feet like a snake. Tong was going to be in for one hell of a surprise, I mused.

Eventually, the room number, time, duration and fee were all sorted out in reception with hardly a word more being spoken. She was charming and professional; to be honest I'd had more difficulty buying lunch in the past. It was cash up front, though — and 'no funny business'.

Job done, and a few hours later Tong was in my room with the phone in his hand, dialling through to reception. He asked for the number of the central police station.

'Is there a problem?' came the reply from the receptionist.

'No, no,' answered Tong, and then as an afterthought, 'at least, not at the moment.'

He was put through various channels until, clearly, he had reached someone of rank. Pleasantries were exchanged, which is a very Muslim thing to do, although I wondered if the Han Chinese policeman at the other end would normally have bothered. Delicately, Tong broached the subject of Zhou Fung Mu and whether he still worked for the department. There was no recollection of that name. Tong looked at me and held his hand over the receiver.

'Are you sure he was chief of police?'

That's what Wang had said. There was no reason for him to lie.

'What about the PSB?' I asked finally, referring to the Public Security Bureau. They were hard-line police, acting on major criminal investigations: murder, rape, hijacking, business fraud. Tong swallowed hard and continued the conversation, but now he was answering more questions than he was asking. Once more, he put his hand to the receiver.

'They're curious to know why you are looking for this man.'

I couldn't tell them the truth. So I made up something on the spot.

'Tell them a distant relative has died and left him some money.'

'How much?'

'A million yuan.'

Tong shook his head. 'Too little. Make it ten,' he said.

While this didn't exactly dampen their curiosity, it did enough to get them to be more helpful — everyone likes a happy inheritance story. The police gave Tong the name and extension number of someone at the PSB, but when we got through to him the name Zhou Fung Mu still drew a blank. I was two calls down and none the wiser.

'Maybe he retired,' said Tong.

'Maybe, but even a retired chief of police would still be remembered.'

Afterwards, I sat in my room alone, feeling miserable. It was getting dark outside. At least someone was smiling, I thought, two floors up in room 402. To shake this particularly graphic mental image out of my head, I imagined how simple this search would be back in my own country. If you wanted to find anyone, you just sat in front of a computer and searched. Seconds later you'd be looking at either their Facebook page, their Twitter site, their Tumblr feed, or any number of other social-media channels. There was a myriad of ways to locate a person, all thanks to the great and mighty Google. If only, I thought, there was something like that in …

'Oh my God,' I said out loud. 'Baidu!'

My back pocket still contained Xu Qing's email address. I went downstairs to where there was a free Internet café, logged on to Hotmail and sent her a quick message. Like any good teenager, she was online and responded within 15 minutes. Her reply was emphatic. In the subject line it read: *Found him!*

Underneath was a link to a small paragraph from a Ganzhou newspaper, honouring the retirement of the city's most senior traffic officer, Mr Zhou Fung Mu, after a lifetime of service. Xu Qing had translated the most important facts and put them in her email. He had, she wrote, retired 10 years ago and now lived in an apartment block that housed important government figures. She knew this because on Baidu there was another story of a retired traffic police chief winning first prize at the Ganzhou Home for Retired Servicemen's annual flower show.

I wrote back asking if there was a picture and she said there was, but only of the winning plant, a rare pink camellia.

Signing off, she wrote, 'Good luck!'

Making her way home as evening falls, near Yudu

TWENTY-ONE

IN THE MORNING, ON A CLEAR, BLUE, CLOUDLESS DAY, IT WAS raining: water dripped from hundreds of air-conditioning units mounted on the outer walls of buildings and fell upon the footpaths. Commuters either ducked and dodged the drops or carried umbrellas. I opted for the former approach and found my way to the city's battlements on the banks of the river Gan. It was dammed upstream by a weir and the surface was so still that a pontoon bridge had been constructed across it. Men with carts transported coal bricks along its length, destined for Ganzhou's restaurant kitchens. Zigzagging between them came a man on a moped with a baby at his feet, facing backwards in a car seat.

Behind me in a park, old men and women performed their tai chi, as if waltzing with invisible partners. Interestingly, these slow, precise movements are taught to the very young using a rhyme:

I have all this. (Arms out in front, palms up.)

Some for him. (Moving weight to the left and appearing to make an offering.)

And some for him. (Moving right and repeating the gesture.)

Now, nothing ('mei ola') do I have. (Returning to the centre, palms up, ready to begin again.)

I had discovered the location of the retirement home, which was a bus ride away on the outskirts of town. The bus stop was down by the river and eventually I found the right bus and climbed aboard. I showed the address to the driver and he nodded assuredly. We then travelled south, over the river and through a dirty industrial precinct that belched steam and smoke, until row upon row of apartment buildings came into view. The driver gestured for me to get off and pointed to the nearest one.

The exterior was dotted with the obligatory air-con units as well as washing lines on every floor, festooned with assorted knickers, pants and singlets that floated in the warm, uprising air. I found the entrance and scanned the letterboxes, hoping to see something I could recognise. Nothing stood out, however, although at least this early reconnoitre meant I knew where to come the next day, when Tong would be free to act as translator again. He was in my debt still and, given the huge grin he had worn over breakfast, I had no doubt he would be up for it.

I decided to walk back into town, sticking to the back streets as much as possible. Along the way I came across an old hotel where a wedding was taking place. Someone had set off firecrackers in the main lobby and the deafening noise drew me to its door. At that moment the bride and groom, she resplendent in her shiny white dress and he in a smart grey suit, emerged and ran past me giggling to a next-door supermarket. Moments later, they returned, proudly waving a box of condoms. I was invited to join the line-up for the wedding photographs, forevermore a strange outsider in a photo album, tacked on the end of a raucous, cheering mob. When the disco music started and the line dancing began, I slunk out the back and continued to the river, crossing over via the pontoon bridge. The wind had risen suddenly and was quite strong, whipping up whitecaps on the water and sending small waves crashing against the side of the bridge, so that it bent in the middle. People carrying large cane baskets on their heads took them down and carried them protectively, in case they were ripped from their grasp. At one point an even more ferocious squall came through and formed a mini-tornado right in front of me, which caught at my clothing and stung my eyes. I ducked down on the planks and stayed there for what seemed an age as the tempest roared around me. It was so strong that it picked up a small goat and tossed it into the river; fortunately, it was still tied to its owner by a slender rope, and was eventually hauled back onto the bridge.

Later that night at the bar, I said to Tong, 'What about that wind?'

'What wind?' he asked, a little bemused. 'Today has been beautiful.'

TWENTY-TWO

The retired policeman was watching TV from his armchair beside an open window. A breeze blew the lightweight curtains out towards him and the fabric caressed his slippered feet. He didn't look up but kept his eyes fixed on the screen, which was showing a news report. The reporter was on the coast and a grey, wind-whipped sea reared up behind her. There were people in high-visibility jackets and an ambulance parked with its lights flashing.

I stood for a full minute before asking Tong what was happening.

'A typhoon hit Fujian province two days ago. Many fishermen lost their lives, but one has been found floating out in the sea.'

'In his boat?'

Just then the reporter began talking to a small, wiry, exhausted-looking man with grey stubble on his chin. He had a blanket round his shoulders and was being helped into the ambulance by two policemen. She managed to thrust her microphone at him and he looked startled momentarily, before finding the strength to smile at the camera and speak. It was as if he'd been waiting to tell his story and now, at last, he had an audience.

'No,' Tong replied. 'It's a miracle. The fisherman says he clung to a branch for a day after the storm, but then it began to sink under his weight. On the second day the dolphins came.'

'Dolphins?'

I looked at the screen and, as if on cue, the old man being interviewed nodded his head and smiled a gap-toothed smile. His hand appeared from under the blanket and grabbed the microphone shakily, so that he could speak more clearly into it.

'He says there were many of them and they kept him afloat all through the day and night, until the rescue craft spotted him in the water.'

'What else?' I asked.

'That's it,' replied Tong. 'He keeps saying the same thing over and over: "The dolphins saved my life. The dolphins saved my life." It's an amazing story, don't you think?'

The old fisherman was being pushed into the ambulance backwards. Slowly retreating, he managed a final wave before the doors slammed shut. The reporter turned back to the camera and, in the time-honoured fashion, signed out and handed back to the main studio. For a few seconds we saw her standing there, saying nothing and continuing to smile into the camera as the wind blew her hair sideways. Then the screen went blank.

I turned in the direction of the armchair to see the former policeman's outstretched hand holding the remote, finger still on the 'off' button. He then placed the remote on the floor and peered at us over the top of his glasses. For the first time I got a good look at him. He was in his mid-seventies but looked like he still kept himself in shape: he had neither a potbelly nor withered arms, the usual hallmarks of age or excess. Quite the opposite in fact: the gentleman I now faced, and had come so far to meet, appeared neither bent nor bowed but held himself stiff and straight, in military fashion. When he stood up it was with one swift movement, and when he walked towards me his stride was strong and well balanced, if a little slow. He was taller than me, but not by much, so I guessed that made him about 180 centimetres, which is exceedingly lofty in China. His handshake was firm, though he didn't squeeze hard as some men feel the need to do in order to make a point or a show of strength. This person, whose eyes were now looking deep into mine, had no need to make such gestures; he already had an air of strength and authority about him.

'I am Zhou,' he said calmly, 'and you are very insistent.'

I couldn't tell if this was a compliment or a reprimand. True, I had been obstinate in my efforts to talk to him, refusing on several occasions that morning to take no for an answer. Through Tong, I had made contact with his housekeeper and she, via the apartment building's intercom, had batted away our requests for a meeting. But in the end, my persistence had won out.

Zhou directed us to a pair of upright chairs opposite his armchair and we sat down, listening to the noise of tea being prepared in the kitchen by his housekeeper. She had let us into the apartment just a few minutes before and had made us wait while the news report was on, her forefinger to her lips, requesting silence. She was about 40, short and rather round, but had a warm and caring nature about her that came to the fore when she was attending to Zhou. I discovered later that she had been working for him for many years, ever since his wife had died of cancer. There was a photo of a good-looking woman in a silver frame on the table beside him and, when he took off his glasses and placed them there, he ran his fingertips down the frame lightly.

With Tong as my translator, we started to chat.

'Do you have a recorder?' he asked.

'No, I don't, I'm sorry,' I said, wishing at the same time that I had bought one just for this meeting.

'Then what kind of journalist are you?'

Rather shamefully, I had played the BBC journalist card again in order to get through Zhou's door. It was my last throw of the dice, and it had worked. Fortunately, I had brought a notepad and pen.

'I don't trust machines,' I replied, turning to a fresh page.

Zhou nodded sagely: 'Ah, I see.'

Because I sensed that my time with Zhou was going to be short, I quickly outlined the story I was working on, regarding the disappearance of Little Mao. It seemed to take him by surprise, but then his calm demeanour swiftly returned.

'You see, I'm a writer with an interest in a missing person.'

'You find lost people,' he said. 'Tell me, what if these people don't want to be found?'

'I would respect their privacy, of course. But I wouldn't know to do that until they told me, or I read a sign on their door that said I'm not wanted.'

He smiled and laughed for the first time.

'True,' he nodded. 'So I gather you think I am connected to this person. Otherwise you wouldn't be in my living room.'

'That's what they seem to believe.'

He leant forward in his seat slightly.

'Who is "they"'?

'Everyone,' I lied. 'In fact, I met a man in Ruijin who was convinced you had …'

I stopped for some reason and he leant forward a little more, clasping his hands between his knees.

'Go on,' he said.

I wasn't about to blurt it out. Saying he'd killed the son of Chairman Mao would have bought us an exit ticket very quickly.

'… had information relating to his death.'

'His death?'

He clapped his hands suddenly and leant back in his chair, chuckling softly.

'I am sorry, this journey of yours is wasted. There is not a shred of truth in any of the things you say. So let me tell you the truth, just so that you don't feel too disappointed.'

His housekeeper brought in some Chinese tea, which she poured into small, blue-and-white ceramic cups from a matching teapot with a cane handle. As she did this, Zhou spoke of his childhood. He had been born in 1932 and raised by foster parents from an early age. They were hard-working farmers he said, but loving parents. He had done well at school and ended up joining the police, got married, had one child — a son — worked hard all his life and eventually climbed to a senior position in the police force before retiring.

'Unlike the one you were proposing, it's not that interesting a life,' he said with a shrug.

I asked him if he had joined the Communist Party and he threw the answer back at me.

'Of course I joined,' he said. 'Everyone did.'

It wasn't quite as convincing a response as I had expected. There was something open-ended about it, as if his membership might have been less than voluntary. However, I didn't want to annoy him, so we talked about his family, his son, who was in the military, and his early years in the police in Ganzhou. It was only when the subject came round to his parents again that the conversation became more stilted.

'Can I ask what happened to your parents?' I asked.

'No.'

'I mean,' I stuttered, 'not your foster parents, but your real parents.'

'My foster parents are my real parents,' he replied, somewhat tersely. 'Either way, all of them are dead.'

'I'm sorry,' I replied.

'Don't be,' he said. 'They died over 40 years ago serving their country. That's all that matters.'

I did a quick calculation in my head. That meant they had died in the 1960s, during Mao's massively catastrophic Great Leap Forward, a time of huge unrest and famine in which millions of Chinese perished. Had they been caught up in that turmoil? Would I be game enough to ask? As it turned out, I didn't get the chance.

Zhou cut the meeting short by saying he was tired and that he hoped I would have a safe journey home. His housekeeper was summoned and we were politely escorted out. On the landing outside Zhou's apartment, Tong expressed his doubts.

'He's hiding something,' he said finally.

The battlements that surround Ganzhou

TWENTY-THREE

Around the corner was the old hotel I had stumbled across the day before. It was quiet now, with no sign of the wedding guests, although there were flower petals floating in the gutter outside. We walked in looking for a drink and found the bar was open. They served Chinese beer and spirits and a strange green liquid inside a bottle that also contained a gutted reptile.

'Lizard wine,' said Tong. 'Have you tried it?'

'No.'

'Then don't,' he muttered. 'Terrible stuff.'

The bar occupied a corner of a large, ornate room with high ceilings, gold Corinthian pillars and great swathes of red carpet. Someone had spilt something in the middle and a woman was on her knees, rubbing at it with a soft brush and soapy water. Gold-painted chairs and tables were stacked to one side, waiting to be put away in storage. Aside from ourselves, there were three men drinking cheap whisky and talking in loud voices that suggested this wasn't their first round, as well as, at another table, a group of older men who sat quietly round a bottle of Napoleon brandy and watched the other table's revelry disapprovingly over the top of their spectacles.

We settled in at one end of the bar and ordered a large bottle of Tsingtao beer, then reviewed the events of that afternoon with Zhou Fung Mu. Tong was convinced that not all was quite right with the retired cop.

'Richard,' he said, 'in my business you get a feeling for people. Some of them will tell you they'll pay on time and you know in your bones they will. Others will tell you the same, but you can tell it may be months before you see a single yuan. My feeling here is that Zhou is saying one thing but thinking another. He's holding something back.'

'You believe he did have something to do with the boy's death?'

'I don't know. But when you brought up the subject it caught him out, just for a second. It was like he wasn't expecting it.'

Tong couldn't be any more specific, so we left it at that and poured the cool beer into small glasses. The first bottle went quickly, so we ordered another. After a third and a fourth we'd tired of beer and moved onto brandy.

'I thought Muslims couldn't drink,' I said, slurring slightly after an hour.

'This one does,' he smiled.

I hadn't had much to drink in months and, perhaps unwisely, I was knocking it back like water. I remember joining the vocal group of men and challenging them to drink the lizard wine. It was brought to the table and the challenge was accepted; fresh glasses appeared and the cap from the bottle was ripped off and thrown away. But what happened after that is still a blur; it was as if the lights went out.

The next morning I woke up in my hotel room, as sick as a

dog and cursing my stupidity. I couldn't recall anything of the night before. When I ran into Tong later that day, however, he filled in the gory details, much to his amusement.

'I'm really sorry,' I groaned.

'Don't worry,' he said. 'It happens to all of us. It was a great night. Incredible really.'

'I'm not sure about that,' I protested weakly.

'You can't remember?'

I shook my head. Tong was grinning from ear to ear.

'Then you don't recall who else came into the bar? You were talking to her for about an hour.'

'Who?'

'Zhou's housekeeper, that's who.'

According to Tong, the housekeeper had come to collect her drunken husband from the bar and found us all together. She'd stayed herself and had apparently knocked back a few rice wines in the process, thereby loosening her tongue on the subject of her employer. A clearly more sober Tong had had the smarts to ask some rather pertinent questions, for which the answers were soon forthcoming.

'And?' I prompted.

'You're not going to believe this,' he replied.

'Try me.'

'She believes — and in fact so do a lot of people round here — that Zhou *is* the boy.'

'What?!'

'Crazy world, huh? Zhou is roughly the right age, he was raised by foster parents, and he even looks a bit like Mao, if you ask me. He's certainly the right height.'

I sat down. This was all too much to take in, and my head was throbbing incessantly as if being pummelled by a thousand pile-drivers. On the other hand, I couldn't have been happier.

I stammered, 'But the journalist in Ruijin said the boy was dead and insinuated that Zhou knew all about it.'

'Maybe,' said Tong, 'what your friend meant was that Zhou had killed Little Mao by denying he was that person.'

'Which would explain why Zhou laughed when I talked about the boy in the past tense. He was enjoying the fact that he knew he was very much alive. Not only that, he was in the room!'

When the excitement died down, one thing that didn't make any sense was why Zhou would deny it. I was mulling this over, unsuccessfully trying to piece the puzzle together, when Tong suddenly sat upright.

'It's obvious,' he said.

Tong then outlined a theory that possibly explained Zhou's dilemma. His parents had died in the Great Leap Forward, which was Mao's great plan to lead China into an industrial age, but which instead resulted in disaster. If Zhou was Little Mao, then his father had killed his foster parents.

'Do you see it now?' Tong asked excitedly. 'How would you feel if the people who had brought you up, who gave you everything in life — food, water, education, warmth and love — were then taken from you? And how would you feel if you knew that it was all because of one man — your father?'

The weight of this man's misery could now be clearly seen, as well as the reason for his reluctance to acknowledge any connection with Mao. I sensed hatred too. So many lives had been harmed through Mao's own burning ambition and his Communist ideology, and yet here was one victim that no one could have predicted: his own son.

Tong was the first to speak: 'So what do you want to do now?'

'First things first, something for this,' I said, massaging my temples. 'Then, let's go and see if we can talk to him one last time.'

TWENTY-FOUR

In my library at home I had read what little there was available on He Zizhen. The information I found described her as a formidable young woman in her own right, even before she'd met and married Mao. Intelligent, quick-witted and blessed with a determination to make a better life not just for herself, but also for her people, she was also someone for whom family was everything. Their marriage was a union of two revolutionaries, but when the march ended and the Revolution approached its successful climax, they fought each other more than they did the Nationalists. Mao's interest in other women was something He Zizhen could not accept. She was not a political wife in that regard, who might turn a blind eye to a powerful husband's infidelities. To Yan'an in 1937, where the marchers had made a home in the caves of Shaanxi province, there came pretty young things from the cities, who caught Mao's eye with their lipstick and fanciful ways. The marriage was as good as over when He Zizhen used her fists against Agnes Smedley, a young and attractive American journalist whose interest in Communism in China extended to a flirtation with its leader. Mao, who probably felt his new and powerful position warranted a different kind of partner, then had He Zizhen sent away to Moscow for 'treatment'. It was true she had suffered injuries on the Long March that would plague her for years afterwards, and the sadness connected to 'Little Mao' had damaged her mentally, but really it was just a way to remove her from the scene.

Naturally this further deprived He Zizhen of opportunities to look for her missing son, so the years she spent in Moscow did her more harm than good. By the time she returned in 1947, Mao had already divorced her and married Lan Ping. Though He Zizhen later became the chair of a women's union south of Shanghai in Zhejiang province, a life in Beijing politics was never possible. It's likely she spent the rest of her years wondering what might have been. And almost certainly the question that would have troubled her the most, right up until her death in Shanghai in 1984, where she lived alone, was what had happened to Little Mao?

Back in my hotel room I rummaged through my bag in search of painkillers, found two and knocked them back with a swig of water. I was about to zip the bag up again when I suddenly noticed the tiny silver heart, neatly sewn into the inner lining so that it wouldn't be knocked about or broken. The bag was an old and trusted one, and I recalled many years before carefully sewing that heart in place. It was plastic, no larger than the size of a child's little fingernail, and came from a Christmas cracker my wife and I had opened a long time before in our West London flat. It was a part of us that I carried around — secretly, quietly, almost without knowing — and each time I bought a new travel bag I'd unpick that heart and sew it into its new home. Sometimes I feared I might forget to do that, and the heart with all its memories might be lost to the rubbish heap, or to a new owner who might consider it worthless and have it cut out.

As my thoughts returned to He Zizhen, I realised how trivial such fears were in comparison to the scale and severity of her loss. She must have suffered enormously. I wondered then what Zhou Fung Mu would think if he knew the level of He Zizhen's despair at his disappearance. If he really was her son, would that not help him find forgiveness and break the trap he was in? The knowledge of her love might be the lifeline to rescue him from hate.

TWENTY-FIVE

In the late afternoon, as the shadow of the ancient city walls creeps ever eastwards, Tong and I find him waiting for us in his apartment.

'I knew you would come,' he says at the door.

His housekeeper has apologised and told him all he needs to know. There is a philosophical note to his voice, as if he finally has to confront the demons that simply won't leave him alone.

He invites us in and we sit in the same chairs as before. He notices me stealing a glance down the hall to the kitchen where there is a notable absence of noise.

'It's her day off,' he says, without being asked.

I begin by apologising for the interruption, but he stops me halfway through.

'Remember yesterday, when I asked you about people not wanting to be found? And you said you would respect their privacy. Well, I am asking you for that privacy. No photographs, no names, no story in the papers — at least while I am alive. Can you promise me that?'

I think long and hard about this, as it means giving up so much of what I've been working for. But then I agree.

'Once I'm gone you can do as you want. It can be your story. But, for the moment, it is mine. Do you understand this?'

Again, I nod in acceptance of his conditions.

He places his hands on his knees: 'Then let's begin.'

* * *

Zhou Fung Mu gave me his life story that day, which is one of the most haunting stories I've ever heard. Sometimes I had to remind myself this was real and not a fairy tale. He talked of a China long ago and of a delightful childhood, including days spent gathering wild mushrooms with his adopted mother to make broth or working the oxen behind the plough with his adopted father. Though the family was of peasant class, he was schooled at home because his mother was a teacher. At first, he wanted to be a teacher also, but there was no money for university and so he had simply continued to work the land into his mid-twenties. When the local Communists commandeered the farm during the Great Leap Forward, it coincided with several years of severe drought. Never had he hated anyone as much as he did the Communist soldiers who came and emptied the family's stores of rice. With no seed to sow and no food to eat, his mother and father succumbed to a plague in the winter that followed.

Now alone, he ventured into the city and eventually found work with the police. He was tall and strong after years of farming, and these physical qualities earned him the respect of his colleagues, as well as a number of promotions that placed him in positions of ever-increasing authority. Once, on meeting the local Communist Party leader, he recognised him as one of those thieving Communist soldiers from years before. Emboldened with liquor, the Party leader boasted of his skill as a wrestler, so Zhou challenged him to a bout and, in the ring, snapped both his arms like twigs.

It was around this time that people started remarking how similar he was to the great Mao, then at the height of his political powers in Beijing, and the story began to spread that Zhou was Mao An Hong. People zeroed in on the genetic traits that seemed to link him to Mao, from the way he walked (a product of both Zhou and Mao being quite tall) to the authoritative way he spoke. People even whispered in hushed tones that his hair was parted in the same fashion.

Despite Zhou's dislike of all these comparisons, he was powerless to stop them from gaining ground. Moreover, to refute them would have been seen as disrespectful, an insult to the most powerful man in all of China, and his many ardent followers — not a wise career move. Only more recently, when the journalist Wang Qiushe had attempted to write the story, had he intervened, using his authority to have the article suppressed. I immediately thought of Wang in his hospital bed: his voice had been removed in more ways than one. For a brief moment I shuddered at the thought that this 'suppression' had gone further than mere censorship. What if Zhou had somehow contributed to Wang's cancer — by having him poisoned, for example? Somehow I doubted he had that in him but, nevertheless, it was a cautionary reminder not to step on the toes of this man, no matter how old he was.

'So you do not think you're the lost son of Mao?' I asked.

He sighed, and then after a lengthy pause said. 'I am Zhou Fung Mu, the only son of Zhou Long and Zhou Na, raised in the fields of Jiangxi province. Like many from that time, my birth parents gave me away in 1934, the same year the Long March began. I was just two, but whether my real parents were "Long Marchers" I can't be sure, though it does seem likely. According to the Communist Party I am simply a boy of China, and when I die I will return to those same fields to enrich the soil with my bones.'

'I hope that doesn't happen for a long time yet,' I said.

'You may wish that,' he replied graciously, 'but my body believes differently.'

He reached out to the photograph of his wife and touched the glass lightly.

'Tell me,' he asked suddenly, changing the subject, 'do you like flowers?'

'Of course,' I replied.

His face brightened. 'Then come with me.'

We followed Zhou down the stairs outside his apartment to the ground floor, where a heavy wooden door opened onto a path to the rear of the building. There we found he'd built a garden with neatly tended rows of vegetables. Beside this was a greenhouse whose many panes of glass could be individually opened to manually control the temperature. Inside we stepped onto bare flagstones that were cool to the touch. Wooden shelves carried a weight of gardening equipment: trowels, forks, gloves, a grafting knife, seed trays and a bag of fertiliser. In the middle of the floor was a line of plain terracotta pots, each of which contained the stem of a plant, no more than 30 centimetres high, which had been neatly grafted and covered with a plastic bag. At the far end of the greenhouse was a larger, more ornate pot that contained Zhou's prize camellia.

'It belonged to my wife.'

He told us that in China the camellia symbolises the long-lasting union of two hearts. The petals are female, while the green sepal that holds them in place is seen as male. Unlike other flowers, when the bloom is over they both fall to the ground together, as one.

'But she went before me, many years ago,' he said sadly.

He had taken up his wife's passion for growing camellias and had learnt to graft different species together so that one camellia tree could have two different types of flower. I told him that in a cottage we used to live in there were two camellia trees planted so close they had fused together and every summer the branches were filled with flowers of two distinct colours, pink and red.

'Beautiful,' he said softly, before adding: 'Are you married?'

'Yes. For many years now.'

'And you love her still?'

'I do,' I replied.

He shuffled his feet around so that he could turn to face me. For the first time that day he was smiling — a broad, contented kind of smile.

'Then,' he said, 'never let her go.'

He pulled out some wooden boxes so that Tong and I could sit while he perched on a stool of his own making. He'd taken an old broomstick handle and cut it into three equal lengths, used smaller pieces of wood to keep the legs apart, then tied the top end together with hemp and inserted that into a hole in the middle of a wooden seat. The parts that stuck up through the hole he had cut off and sanded flat. He said somewhat apologetically that he was a policeman not a carpenter, but I could tell he was a little of both.

'Are you happy now?' he asked. 'Now that you know my story.'

'Not quite,' I replied.

He raised his eyebrows and sat a little taller on the stool. I felt his mood shift a little, away from the light and back towards the darkness inside him.

'I would like you to read something,' I said, offering to him several pages of paper covered in Chinese writing that I had printed out at the hotel.

He took them from my hand and reached for his reading glasses, fumbling to get them open.

'What is this?' he queried, not without a note of irritation.

'This is the only historically accurate account I can find that describes the events after the Long March and what happened to He Zizhen, your mother.'

The papers trembled in his hands, though I wasn't sure whether that was due to old age, anger or some other emotion. He seemed to be reading sections then skipping past others; finally he flicked to the end and stopped.

'Why are you doing this?' he asked.

'Because I think it might help.'

'Help. Help with what?'

'The bitterness you feel towards her. Mao I can understand, after what he did to you and your family, but her? She just wanted her son back. She was just a mother in the end, distraught at the loss of her child and doing whatever she could to find him again — because she loved him, more than anything else on earth.'

For a moment he seemed to shrink in stature. His shoulders dropped and the pages dangled limply from his fingers. Finally he spoke.

'If this is true, if I am who you think I am, what of it? This is the past. No one cares anymore. She is gone, he is gone, my wife is gone; they're all dead. And this is not proof of anything,' he said, waving the papers in the air abruptly.

'I know,' I replied. 'It's not proof of whether you are Little Mao or not. That would require DNA testing and a whole lot more besides. But if there is a part of you that believes you may be him, and you've spent your life hating your birth mother for giving up on you, then here is the proof.'

'Proof?' he demanded. 'Of what?'

'That she never did.'

I got up suddenly because I realised everything I'd come to say had been said. If I'd had a part to play in all of this, it was completed. Now I felt I had intruded enough on the life of this old man. I left him in his garden shed, clutching the papers and surrounded by flowers of love.

TWENTY-SIX

Dale, the university researcher at Chengdu, hadn't given me his telephone number, but I did have his email address. I wrote to him and begged a favour. There was a young girl who was bright, ambitious and full of academic promise — would he be willing to give her some scholarly advice? His reply came a day later saying that would be fine.

'What is she hoping to study?' he wrote.

'English lit,' I replied.

'Perfect. Send her my way.'

That afternoon I despatched a separate email to Xu Qing, introducing her to Dale and telling her about his offer of assistance. There were no promises, but ... 'Sometimes,' I wrote at the end of the email, 'it's not what you know, but who.'

Once again she was quick to respond and her email seemed like she was excited. Chengdu was one of her big three universities. Having a contact at one of them was just what she needed, she wrote. Her parents were very happy and wanted to meet me. She concluded her email with a question: 'Are you returning to Ruijin?'

Ruijin was a long bus ride east and I had a plane to catch

from Shanghai. There wasn't enough time for me to make it there and back before taking my train. Sadly, I told her, it would have to wait for another occasion. But I knew full well that the chances of me returning this way were slim. The wheels of life never stop turning, not for anyone, and I had my own personal challenges to pursue. And, most of all, my own family to think about. I hadn't seen them in what felt like ages.

I looked at my watch: it was 3 p.m. Back home, dinner would be on the way and two cats would be standing by their bowls looking hopeful. I decided to make a Skype call home in the hope that someone would answer.

The soft burr of the ring tone filled the void between us. On this journey, keeping in touch had been easier thanks to the way China's youth were opening Internet cafés almost everywhere and anywhere, even though the connections were sometimes a little unreliable. At the current pace of change, China would soon join the very top rank of hi-tech industrialised nations. Yet, despite the usefulness of these modern communication technologies, I couldn't help but feel nostalgic for the old, dark and mysterious version of this country — a place where a traveller could literally disappear. Part of me missed that world, with its illicit currency dealings, black-market train tickets and the constant stares of a population who'd never before seen a white face.

The line must have been ringing for a full minute before a voice answered.

'Hellooo,' said Issie. 'Is that the Daddy-O calling?'

The screen was black, the signal not strong enough for video, but her voice was clear.

'Hey there,' I said. 'What's for dinner?'

'I'm making pasta. It's just me here. Mum's dropping Tom off at a party.'

'Is she now?'

'Where are you? China still?'

'Yes, but home soon, okay?'

She squealed and I pictured her on the swivel chair at the computer. When she was little she would sit there for ages, grabbing the desk and using it to make the seat spin.

'Will you write the book when you get back?'

'Maybe,' I said, remembering my promise to Zhou. 'It might take a while to finish though.'

'Lazy!' she teased. 'Like you always say to me, all you need to do is keep putting one foot in front of the other. Don't stop, no matter what.'

'I'll bear that in mind, O Wise Omnipotent One.'

After we'd hung up, there wasn't much else I could do but say a few goodbyes in Ganzhou. Tong had been a godsend, and without his help none of the subtleties of my conversations with Zhou would have been translated so accurately. His conference over, he was flying out of Ganzhou and heading home to Shanghai.

'Come and stay if you have time,' he offered.

I said I would see.

Time was tight and the overnight train from Ganzhou could not be late if I was to make my flight. Fortunately, unlike some, this Chinese train maintained a Germanic timetable.

Before boarding, however, there was one last surprise no one could have predicted. I was waiting on the platform when a hand touched my shoulder. I spun round to find Zhou Fung Mu standing there, supported by a wooden cane. He was dressed up in a smart but casual fashion, tall and straight with his hair neatly parted in a way I'd seen many a time on someone else, someone infinitely better known. The hotel had told him where to find me, and he had a gift to give me. Without Tong's translation I thought I might have trouble communicating, but in the end he had nothing to say. He merely reached into the breast pocket of his jacket and took out a small see-through plastic box in which he'd carefully placed a single pink camellia. We shook hands and smiled at each other as the voice over the Tannoy announced my train was leaving. The driver released the brakes and the train lurched forward. The carriages clanked noisily and a railway official shouted at me to get on. I stood on the first step and looked back, one hand on the door and the other holding a flower. But Zhou Fung Mu was already walking back the way he had come. Without turning, and as if he knew I would be watching, he raised his right hand and waved.

* * *

I shared a sleeper compartment with a couple of female university students heading back to their studies after a mid-term break. One was doing a marketing degree and hoped to work for a big multinational like Unilever. She was doing her final year thesis on the 'Social Impact and Efficacy of Skin-whitening Products'.

'How's it going?' I enquired.

'Very good,' she said, extending a slender arm and examining the pale, slightly off-white pigment of her own skin. 'You can really see the difference.'

'I meant your thesis.'

'Oh that,' she replied, and then giggled with her hand over her mouth.

Not for the first time I reflected on the fact that the world's largest Communist government would soon be presiding over the world's most capitalist population.

'I like your flower,' she said, and without waiting for approval, picked up the box and opened it.

'From your wife?' she smiled.

'Not exactly,' I replied.

'Ah, your girlfriend.'

'Not that either,' I said. 'Just someone.'

'Ah, I see. But they are Chinese friend.'

'How can you tell?'

'The note is written in Pinyin.'

'What note?'

'This one,' and she showed me the small piece of paper, which I had completely overlooked at the bottom of the box. On it were two Chinese characters, written clearly and simply in an elegant hand.

'Can you tell me what it says?' I asked.

'Sure. It's written *Xie xie*,' she said.

Even I didn't need help with the translation. It's one of the most often heard sayings in all of China. It simply means 'thank you'.

* * *

In the morning, Shanghai loomed out of a smog-grey sky and I found myself back where I had started, fighting through the crowds, trying to dodge the hawkers who did their utmost to sell me a Chairman Mao key ring.

'Hey mister! Look good on your Mercedes.'

'I don't have a Mercedes.'

'Aw, too bad. Even my mum drives one. Here,' he said, dangling the gaudy trinkets before my eyes. 'I give you freebie.'

I spent the last day in China being a Red Traveller and going to see Mao's former residence in Shanghai. The two-storey building was hard to find, at the end of an alleyway surrounded by a busy shopping complex, situated in a shaded *shikumen* courtyard on a street called Maoming Lu. According to the sign out front, this was where Mao spent his longest visit to Shanghai in 1924 and it's the only one of his former abodes open to the public. I suspected that, like so many exhibits in China that honour the former Leader, this would be yet another showcase for Communist propaganda rather than a genuine historic site. Happily, that feeling was alleviated slightly when, in a downstairs room, I came face to face with a quite convincing wax figure of Mao himself, seated at a writing desk with his body turned to face the door. It felt as if I had interrupted him in whatever scholarly Marxist endeavours he had been engaged in. I had to stop myself from apologising for the intrusion, such was the life-like nature of the figure. Perhaps it was only right he should feel imposed upon. I had pried deep into his private life, uncovered things about him that were unbecoming to say the least, and now here I was — an audience of one, in his presence.

What would he have said to me, given the chance? Would he have tried to defend his treatment of He Zizhen, or his decision not to search for their missing son, Mao An Hong? He might have claimed that his attention lay elsewhere, that he was consumed by matters of greater importance. But what can be more important than a child?

I imagined Mao growling a reply to this: *'You do not understand. A revolution is not a dinner party.'*

'Touché,' I thought.

There came a noise behind me, like the shuffling of slippered feet, and I realised I was no longer alone. The middle-aged Chinese man standing in the hallway was curious to know what I thought of the wax figure. I told him it was very good and he smiled proudly, then tapped his chest.

'They are mine,' he said, and I noted a slight American accent. 'I make them from silicone. I used to produce Hollywood figures like Charlie Chaplin and Marilyn Monroe. You should have seen my Harry Potter! But Chairman Mao was the hardest of all. There was a lot of pressure to get him just right.'

He wiped an imaginary bead of sweat from his brow and talked about the irony of his life, escaping from China to America in his twenties and then returning decades later to create a model of the man he had been running from. I had to laugh at the strangeness of it all. It was, in the end, a perfectly modern Chinese story.

I put a question to him. He had said 'they' before, which was curious because I'd only encountered the figure of Mao.

He blinked with surprise and sounded disappointed: 'You haven't seen the others?'

He took me to a neighbouring room, where we found them in their eternal repose, carbon copies of mother and child. The woman was young and she was perched on the side of a bed, her hand reaching out gently towards a sleeping baby in a wicker cradle. A sign indicated this was Mao's wife. I asked him which one and he replied that the authorities had requested he commemorate Yang Kahui, Mao's second wife, who had died at the hands of Nationalist soldiers.

'But just between you and me,' he confided in a whisper, 'I actually based the figure on his third wife. She was my favourite of all Mao's companions. A good woman.'

'This is He Zizhen?' I blurted out, almost in disbelief.

He put a finger to his lips and nodded. Suddenly the face looked very familiar. The hair was shoulder length, which matched the old black-and-white photos I'd seen of both women, but particularly He Zizhen. However, the full mouth, button nose and wide eyes were definitely hers. She was prettier than her predecessor, Yang Kahui, who for the most part peered somewhat glumly from her photographs, as if life were a trial. This face on the other hand, was flush with youthful beauty and energy.

'Which means the infant is …?'

We both looked down to where the replica of the child lay, swaddled in a white nightshirt beneath a blanket of navy blue and seemingly sleeping. The black hair looked so real and the tiny facial features were so precise that I almost thought the bedclothes were rising and falling with each breath.

'It is the one she lost,' he replied. 'This is the one they called Little Mao, because he was just like his father.'

It was a while before either of us said anything more. We were both lost in our own private worlds: mine revolving around this remarkable new discovery, while he most probably was simply admiring the brilliance of his handiwork.

'He wasn't, you know,' I said finally, breaking the silence.

'Wasn't what?' he replied.

'Little Mao,' I continued. 'He wasn't at all like his father. Not even a little bit.'

The wax worker looked at me strangely, then laughed uneasily and shrugged his shoulders.

'Everybody's an expert,' he muttered, half under his breath, as he shuffled off to another room.

Perhaps I should have explained so that he might have understood, but I doubt whether he would have believed me. Besides which, it would have taken too long and time was running out.

'Always in a hurry.'

It was Mao again from the room next door, his voice cold like his synthetic skin.

'You run from place to place looking for your ghosts, searching for your answers. But will your book tell the story of my sacrifices in order to build this great and glorious nation? No, it will not! It will tell lies about me, I can tell. I see through you, like I saw through those who tried in vain to stand in my way. Chiang Kai-shek attacked me and lost; the Japanese tried to smash me and failed; the United States of America entered the Korean War in order to break my Communist Party, but they were driven back; even Khrushchev wanted me gone and I defied him! You are nothing in comparison, and the only thing you will share with them all is failure.'

The voice fell silent. Mao's statue of wax stared with eyes of polished glass, daring me to reply. But the only thing I could think to do was to close the door and leave him in his little room, glaring at the walls.

* * *

Later that day I caught the 400-kilometre-per-hour bullet train to the airport, navigated my way through the various official channels and boarded my flight. Next to me on the plane was an Australian man who explained how he'd spent this particular trip collecting old Communist Party propaganda, mostly posters.

'It's funny y'know,' he said, 'they kept having to print new ones showing Mao's latest deputies, because he went through so many: Gao Gang, Liu Shaoqi — they were all senior party officials who met with a sticky end.'

'Do you have a favourite poster?' I asked.

'Easy. It's of a troupe of ballerinas in pointe shoes, balancing on the tips of their toes while holding rifles to their rosy cheeks and peering through the gun sights. Genius! You've gotta love this country sometimes.'

I told him I couldn't agree more. But secretly I knew you could hate it too. There was no getting away from the fact that this country was both fair and foul, polarising in its charms. It could be maddening and marvellous in the space of a single afternoon, triumphant and terrible, beautiful and barbarous in equal quantities. Yet all the while you knew there was no other place on the planet quite like it.

A young woman on her way to work

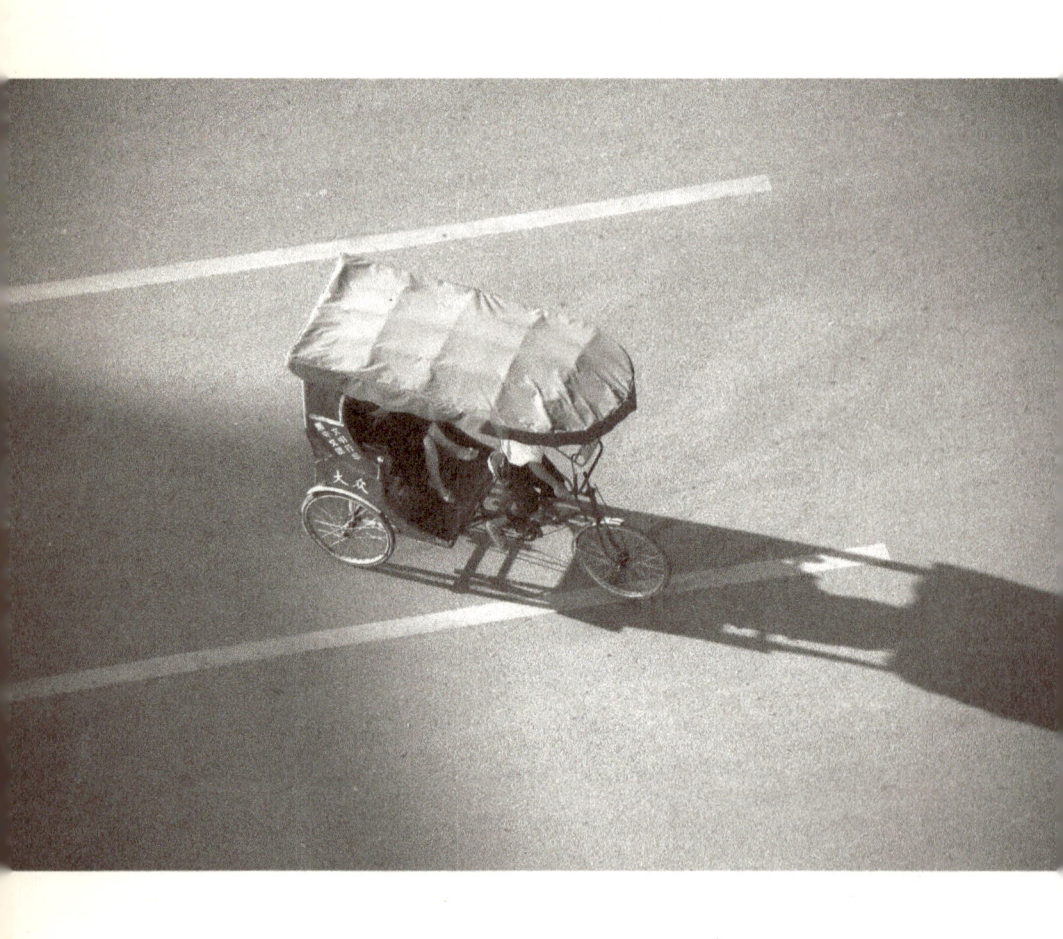

TWENTY-SEVEN

'Think of your readers, Richard,' my editor muttered, half in jest, across the restaurant table. 'Don't keep them waiting.'

He was right: they had every cause for complaint. It had already been five years since I'd returned from China. My teenage children were almost grown up. Tom was at university and Issie in her last year of high school. The garden was littered with the graves of family pets that had come and gone since my return. Where had the time gone? But always I reminded myself of the promise I had made to Zhou Fung Mu, a promise kept secret all this time.

'It's coming along,' I said, trying to sound positive.

'Just finish it!' he cried, his eyes twinkling mischievously. 'God knows, I haven't got all the time in the world.'

No one could have foretold that just a short while later I would be present at his funeral. He told no one of his cancer until the very last moment. The memorial was a standing-room-only event at his home, packed to the gunnels with people who, like me, held him in high regard. Afterwards though, I felt I'd had enough of saying goodbye to people, and hoped it would be the last farewell for a good long while.

But there was to be one more significant death that year.

Quite out of the blue, I received an email from an unknown address — it was just by chance that I fished it out of the junk folder. It was from Tong. He said he hoped that I was well, asked after my family and, in the name of Allah, wished them good fortune. Attached to the email was a local news article from Ganzhou, which quietly recorded the passing of retired traffic police chief Zhou Fung Mu.

I sat at the computer screen and read it several times over.

There was no way of proving what I believed to be true, that I had stumbled upon the last surviving son of the Great Helmsman, who controversially shaped the course of China, if not the world. But somehow that was no longer the point of the journey anymore. I knew I had unearthed a different story, which to me felt even more powerful than that of the Long March or Mao's missing son. This one belonged to He Zizhen, and it was the story of a mother's love for her child, and how that love never diminished, even though it was barely reciprocated in her lifetime. Perhaps now, somehow, somewhere, it might be.

I pictured Zhou Fung Mu, reunited with his beloved wife amongst the camellia flowers that bound them together. But also, just maybe, with someone else — someone who had been waiting to see him again for a very long time.

In the newspaper article, however, there was no mention of Little Mao or He Zizhen.

It was just the way he would have liked it.

EPILOGUE

Shanghai, 1984

The sound of a trolley bus outside her third-floor window woke He Zizhen from a deep sleep and she sat up slowly in her bed. She had been dreaming again, as she did so often these days — or was it more a memory? Yet again it was of that desperate day in Yudu, half a century earlier: the Red Army soldiers shouting for them to prepare to leave, a pervading sense of panic in their voices, as she stole one final embrace with her only son before Mao Zetan carried him away. She remembered the boy's tiny, fearful face, and his hands outstretched towards her. Then there was the aching despair that lasted long into the night and through all the days that followed, as she marched onwards with her comrades, fearing for her son's life far more than her own. What had Mao said to her: that she shouldn't worry, that she would have more children by him eventually? How could he care so little?

He Zizhen lay her aged body back down and thought of Little Mao again, wondering once more what fate had befallen him — and hoping against hope that he had survived. Other, much bleaker images crowded at the edge of her consciousness. She closed her eyes and reminded herself to breathe, long and deep, to not let these dark thoughts gain a foothold in her mind. With each slow breath she concentrated on a vision of her son, seeing him alive and well, first as a child, playing happily in a field with his new family, then growing up with a kind-hearted peasant woman and her husband, learning how to use a plough, how to cut wheat and sow barley seed, and how to watch for the swallows in spring that would herald the best time for planting rice. She saw him become as tall and handsome as his father, as well as smart, and a crack-shot with a rifle, like his mother. And once again, as she had done so many times, she allowed herself to think about finding him and holding him in her arms.

Slowly, into this vision came a soft light that was soon everywhere, all round them, growing stronger as it ran across their hair, along their arms and fingers, dancing on their skin. It pressed them together so closely she could feel his heart beating. It was like the old days before the march, when he would sit on her lap and she'd tell him stories of her parents, of the town where she grew up on the Heshui River, of its still and placid reservoirs where ducks and geese would skim across the water as they landed, the ripples from their wake breaking in small perfect waves against the riverbank. She would tell him about the Revolution too, hoping he might understand how they were trying to create a better, fairer world for them all. How there would be sacrifices, that he might go hungry at times, and that he might not see her for a while. She'd tried to explain that there were people who were angry at them, soldiers — not from their lands but from far away — who would come soon and drive his mother and father out. He'd looked at her with such knowing back then and, with his little hand on her cheek, wiped away her tears.

The light faded as the rumble of Shanghai's traffic floated into her room. All of a sudden the air felt thick and heavy, and she could hear her own breathing becoming louder and more laboured — rasping, rattling, each gasp harder to fight for than the last, until the time came when she could fight no more.

In her final moments, He Zizhen thought she heard voices shouting. From somewhere, orders were being given by the cadre. Donkeys had to be loaded up, horses brought from the stables. The enemy were coming. The rumble of their guns was creeping ever closer. Soon she would be marching on again. And yet, suddenly, none of it mattered anymore.

'Be strong, Little Mao,' she whispered, her wrinkled hands clenched into fists. 'I will find you.'

ACKNOWLEDGMENTS

THIS BOOK WOULD NOT HAVE BEEN POSSIBLE WITHOUT THE SUPPORT of my wife, Elisabeth, and my children, Tom and Issie, who provided love and encouragement throughout this long adventure. I also owe a debt of gratitude to my good friend Michael Gifkens for his literary guidance, to John Daly for his help in selecting photographs for the book, and to Robyn Hamilton for her invaluable research into the life of He Zizhen. Finally, I would like to remember the monks of Thrangu Monastery near Yushu, many of whom lost their lives in the devastating earthquake of 2010. Although Yushu suffered severe damage, Thrangu was almost completely destroyed.